3000 800013 434

St. Louis Community College

W9-DDW-583

WITHDRAWN

WITHDRAWN

THE JAPANESE OVERSEAS

THE JAPANESE OVERSEAS

Can They Go Home Again?

Merry White

THE FREE PRESS
A Division of Macmillan, Inc.
NEW YORK

Collier Macmillan Publishers
LONDON

Copyright © 1988 by Merry White

All rights reserved. No part of this book may be reproduced or transmitted in any form or by any means, electronic or mechanical, including photocopying, recording, or by any information storage and retrieval system, without permission in writing from the Publisher.

The Free Press
A Division of Macmillan, Inc.
866 Third Avenue, New York, N.Y. 10022

Collier Macmillan Canada, Inc.

Printed in the United States of America

printing number
1   2   3   4   5   6   7   8   9   10

Library of Congress Cataloging–in–Publication Data

White, Merry I.
    The Japanese overseas: can they go home again? / Merry White.
        p.   cm.
    Bibliography: p.
    Includes index.
    ISBN 0-02-935091-3
    1. Family—Japan—Psychological aspects. 2. National characteristics, Japanese. 3. Reverse culture shock—Japan. 4. Japanese—Foreign countries—Psychology. 5. Social adjustment. 6. Student adjustment.   I. Title.
HQ682.W48 1988
305.8′956′073—dc19
                                                        87–33836
                                                          CIP

For my parents

Contents

Acknowledgments

In the preparation of this book I was greatly aided by many thoughtful scholars and friends in Japan and the United States. I am especially grateful to Professor Yoshihiro Shimizu, formerly professor of educational sociology at Tokyo University and now at Sophia University in Tokyo, whose considerate attention and advice kept my work in Japan on the right track. Through Professor Shimizu I was able to benefit from the help of Professor Ikuo Arai of the Tokyo Institute of Technology and Mr. Kato Koji of the National Institute for Educational Research. Others who helped me in Japan were Sachiko and Yoshimitsu Ide, Sumiko Iwao, Wakako Hironaka, and the late Kinuko Kubota. Penelope Brown, Hitomai Haga, Junko Shigematsu, Toshiko Muto Ohta, and the staff of the Kaigai Shijo Kyoiku Shinko Zaidan were invaluable aids in research. I would especially like to thank Mrs. Hideko Mitsui of Keimei Gakuen and her late husband Takasumi Mitsui for all the kindness and support they offered during my stay in Japan and after. My greatest assistance in Japan, of course, came from all those who acted as informants and gave many hours of their time to help me understand their society and their experiences.

Ezra Vogel of Harvard University served as my major adviser on this project and provided encouragement, direction, perspective, and friendship. The late Judith Strauch was a tireless and loyal friend and reader of drafts. Nathan Glazer and others at the Harvard Graduate School of Education made helpful suggestions. Sakie Fukushima helped me patiently in my use of Japanese sources and documents. Anna Laura Rosow, Patrick Maddox, Barbara Molony, Howard Spendelow, Ellen Widmer, and many others helped me through many sloughs of despond in the early drafts. John Zeugner and Alice Valentine shared my love of Japan and sharpened my critical perspective, and Alice, who should be considered the godmother of this book, particularly shared with me all the pains and triumphs of years of Japanese language classes. Catherine Lewis, Thomas Rohlen, and Lois Peak read later drafts and helped to sort wheat from chaff. Robert LeVine helped give shape to the view of culture represented here and encouraged me to carry on in this book the work we had begun earlier. I would like to thank Margaret Herzig, my creative and painstaking friend and colleague, who has seen this manuscript from thesis to book and who at the end spent many hours helping me to edit it. She is the "without whom" this book would still be in limbo. Grant Ujifusa, my editor, continued to provide energy and focus to my work as he has in the past, and I am very grateful to him. Finally, I thank my own "international children": Jennifer White, who accompanied me to Japan for the research year, and Benjamin Wurgaft, who was born in the middle of the writing, for they have tolerated and inspired me throughout.

1

Families at Risk

Iki wa yoi, yoi; kaeri wa kowai
[Leaving is good, but it's frightening to return].
                                         —Japanese children's game chant[1]

This chant, which accompanies a playground circle game, conveys some of the costs borne by Japanese who venture abroad. The children unclasp their hands and raise their arms to signal that the one who is "it" may leave freely. Then they grab hands and move together again quickly to prevent the child from getting back inside. The tight closed circle may be taken as a symbol of the exclusion often felt by families returning to Japan.

Japanese families who have gone overseas are caught in a paradoxical culture warp—agents of Japanese international economic growth, they themselves have derived little domestic benefit from their sojourns away from Japan. In fact, these fathers, mothers, and children must bear the brunt of a cultural ambivalence about foreigners that belies Japan's success in the international market.

When these families come home to Japan, they suffer the "crisis of return," a well-publicized and constantly analyzed reentry problem. The crisis—experienced by children in schools, mothers in the community, and fathers in the workplace—requires conscious adjustment and strategizing by individuals and by families. This book is about the people who must negotiate this difficult return from an outward-looking economy to an inward-looking culture.

Rapid modernization has caused a breakdown of traditional social structures and values in many cultures. But—despite perhaps the most dramatically swift rise to industrial success the world has ever seen— Japan does not give much evidence of such a breakdown. Indeed, even as the world expects the costs of modernization to catch up with Japan, few significant rents have yet been spotted in the country's social fabric. One key to the mystery may lie in the fact that Japanese groups—among the most important, the family, community, and workplace—are both adaptive and self-protective. Accordingly, Japan is a "survival culture" whose success is based on the capacity of such groups to ensure their own perpetuation.

The governing concept, the core, of a Japanese group is the idea of the *uchi* (home, inside), a primary place of affiliation. The uchi is where one is taken care of, where one receives support and encouragement, and where one owes one's central commitment and effort. It is where one comes from and where one returns. Although a family home is the central and archetypal uchi, other groups assume the characteristics of an uchi as well, notably the company or place of work. When, for example, a person introduces him- or herself, it is frequently by company name, as in, "I am Tanaka of Mitsubishi."

The uchi protects itself in various ways, most notably by its privacy and exclusivity. Families, communities, and companies monitor members' behavior and performance, and although permanent membership guarantees that only extreme cases of deviation will be openly punished, the rewards of acceptance and the threat of banishment encourage conformity. Especially in times of rapid and turbulent change, the predictability of one's identity in an uchi environment offers essential security and comfort.

There are threats to the individual and to the personal uchi, however. Returnees, for example, may be marked as different, or as having been away too long to be trusted, and may be subtly isolated or directly confronted by the results of their "apostasy." While returnees are not absolutely abandoned by most uchis, they may nonetheless find themselves with permanently flawed identities or isolated within the group as functional but problematic or marginal members. The existence of this cordon sanitaire of Japanese domestic institutions encourages growth and change in the international arena but marks those who implement the desirable as themselves less than fully desirable.

The reentry shock experienced by Japanese overseas employees is a complex object of inquiry. Observers charting Japan's continuing "modernization," in which Japanese organizations are seen as moving awkwardly toward Western models of development, may see it as of ephemeral historical interest. Alternatively, the existence of this shock may signify basic cultural differences that can influence what "modern" means in the world today.

My perspective on the returnees is strongly influenced by an active view of "culture." I do not think that we can regard "culture" as merely exotic manifestations that lend diverse color to the world's societies and provide some local flavor on the menus of a Hilton or Holiday Inn in Frankfurt or Samoa. Instead of such a superficial view, this study affirms the centrality and active power of cultural meaning even in one of the most "modern" societies in the world, Japan. We need to understand basic cultural values and principles of organization to facilitate communication and to improve the uneasy workings of a global economy.

The specific Japanese problems documented will be looked at from several perspectives. First, it offers a way to consider Japanese identity. One can also observe changes in contemporary family structure, corporate organizational dynamics, and cultural conceptions of individual virtues and life chances. All these aspects of life are brought into high relief by the threats to identity created and implied by the internationalization of Japanese people and work.

We will look at the many contexts in which families experience the results of their international sojourn. Chapter 2 outlines the historical experiences of Japanese foreign sojourners, gives an overview of the contemporary setting, and provides a description of a family on the verge of departure from Japan. Chapter 3 paints portraits of three returnee families. Chapter 4 looks at the returnee child in school and Chapter 5 at mothers and fathers in the community and workplace. Finally, Chapter 6 analyzes the broad role of the "border broker" in Japanese organizations and considers the state and prospects of internationalization in Japan.

The Japanese Family Today

A few years ago there was a "movement," both engendered and encouraged by the media and commercial interests, called *maihomu-shugi* (my-homeism). This called for making the family the emotional center of activity and consumption. In this "ideal" family the children happily played electronic games, the father practiced putting on a small, artificial indoor green, and the mother demonstrated her cooking skills in elaborate meals that the family ate together. Although my-homeism sold many toys, do-it-yourself kits, and gourmet cooking utensils, the home itself could never compete with the company and school as arenas of activity. Most of a man's waking hours are spent at work or with colleagues, and most of a child's are spent at school or studying. If the housewife so chose, she might indeed find time to devote to the magnificent meals of the microwave oven advertisements, but she might equally well end by eating them alone.

This compartmentalization of activities was not always a fact of Japanese life. In the past the family served as the unit of economic production, the socializer of children, and the source of an individual's status in the community. Its demands for loyalty and obedience were strong, and membership was permanent. It was a true uchi. But the modern nuclear family, although still very much an uchi, seems to serve only as a place where children are supported and where the breadwinner can relax. It is the locus of an active identity only for the mother, who, through her nurturing support of the others, maintains the household in service to the outside (soto)—to the workplace and school—which has different norms and rules for the behavior and performance of individuals.

The Central Role of the Housewife

With the number of its functions reduced, the Japanese family has emerged as an institution that is strong, flexible, and adaptive. It is based not on the role of the provider-father or on the relationship between husband and wife but on the nurturing, organizing, service role of the mother-housewife, and on her relationship with the children. She alone is completely focused on the tasks and goals of the family, and it is to her that all important domestic decisions and budget matters are referred. In general the responsibility for the house, children, and community activities is hers. The primary roles of other family members are located outside the family, and although their success in those roles is vital to the happiness and security of the family unit, they are not identified primarily by their function within it. They are employees of Company X or students of School Y, working for themselves and their soto groups and not explicitly for Family Z. The housewife, however, works for the uchi and is identified by it, however residual it may have become as a primary group for its other members. She is Z no okusan (the Z housewife)—defined by her role as homemaker to the house of Z.

The returnee housewife may be very much less "in control" of her family's destiny than the woman who has never had to cope with being away. Her role as a mother is strongly affected by the strains the educational system places on her children, and her role as a wife is affected by the difficulties her husband experiences as a corporate returnee. Finally, her role as a member of the community is influenced by the personal changes generated by the overseas experience, by the choices she makes as a result, and by her community's perception of the shift in family members' status in the educational and occupational systems.

Family, School, and Workplace

A closer look at the middle-class family will help us to understand the role of the housewife and the relationships the family maintains with outside institutions—relationships on which the success of readjustment for a returnee family hinges.

Most middle-class families interact with the community at several points. First, the children are members of their school, and the mother belongs to the PTA. Through these relationships the family learns what the outside world expects of children as future members of other social institutions and what it expects of the family as a participant in the children's socialization.[2] The mother acts as a bridge between family and school, a role that requires much time and energy. The school, even at the height of the examination struggle, helps to integrate the mother into her children's education—through the PTA, through conferences with teachers, through advice to parents on how to help their children. The mother supports the children and encourages them to feel that their efforts are important to the family as a whole. She does not use force or overt discipline but (ideally) encourages them to study without alienating them from school or from the family.[3]

The mother knows each child's strengths and weaknesses and thus knows best how to foster each child's desire to work. She must constantly monitor her children's work and must teach her offspring *how* as well as *what* to study. The assumption among mothers is that children need to be encouraged, that study for exams is a cooperative effort, and that without the mother's support, the child cannot perform effectively. Mothers say that there is little choice: They must either be *kyoiku mama* (education mothers) or *shikata ga nai* (there's no help for it) mothers. They see little in between.

The mother is also a bridge to the neighborhood, to ward offices, volunteer citizens' groups, cleanup teams, the retail trade, and to other families. She represents the family on residents' committees and to official and commercial agencies as well. The Western image of the Japanese housewife is of someone who is humble and retiring, but in her own sphere she can be self-reliant, independent and even aggressive. Few women in Japan respond to door-to-door salespeople, public opinion pollsters, or census takers by saying, "I'll have to ask my husband about that." In uchi matters, the housewife is very much in command. She shops and sits at the playground with other mothers to learn and share the lore not just of motherhood but also of the community.

The father, on the other hand, finds himself mostly in the world of business. The father's interest in and involvement with his family are seen as important to his personal well-being; company rhetoric has it that a good worker is supported by a happy family. But if he appears to neglect the work group for family activities, he is accused of being too family oriented, too self-centered, favoring his private affairs over his work. He does, of course, have a vital role in his family—he provides its economic support and social status. However, for the neighborhood, the critical criteria for a successful family are that the mother be a good housewife and that the children do well at school.

For the family, then, the father has an "external" life. The work he does is not well understood. Some women might easily say that their husbands just shuffle papers, which is much less important than raising children. Other women, however, are more deeply involved in their husbands' careers; they listen to their problems and provide encouragement. In neither case do women visit their husbands' offices, and only rarely do they entertain his colleagues or their wives. Exceptions include families living in company housing or those who have been relocated overseas or to regional offices where they have no other affiliations than those made through company connections. In these instances, wives and children of colleagues may socialize with one another, although women say that they are too aware of their husbands' delicate status relationships at work to be truly comfortable with other company wives. Children often have little idea of what their fathers do at work or what their firms do, although even a small child usually knows the *name* of the father's company.

The separation of the father from family matters does not in general create major problems, but in some families it causes strains that cannot be ignored. The father often feels like an outsider, and in extreme cases he may be actively excluded from his wife's sphere. Mothers may sometimes feel insecure about their ability to make decisions. Separated not only from their husbands but from the support of an extended family, they may suffer extreme anxiety. However, it seems that this pattern of role separation, though perhaps exaggerated now, is a fairly long-standing one that does not in itself mar marriage or family life. Japanese families have always centered on parent-child relationships rather than on that between husband and wife. A woman's sense of accomplishment comes primarily from motherhood and not from her relationship with her husband. The children are her responsibility, and the father's long absences from the home provide few opportunities for sustained intimacy between father and child. There is even a saying among Japanese women that the good husband is "healthy and absent."

Partly because of the demands of the examination system and the mother's role as sole support of the studying child, and partly because their other roles in the home are less active and compelling, mothers encourage dependency in their children long into adolescence. So it is that Japanese teachers say that children are spoiled at home and don't know how to take care of themselves. Mothers will confess that their teenage daughters don't know how to make tea or sew on a button and that their college-age sons have never tidied their own rooms or even opened the refrigerator to get themselves a snack. Since the mother's role is centered on nurturance, she is unwilling to minimize her importance to the home by assigning household tasks to children whose energies are, in any case, seen to be better spent in study. By keeping them in a state of relative dependence, she maintains autonomous control of the household. Moreover, in an isolated nuclear family, she relies on the children for companionship and loyalty and is afraid of alienating them by making too many demands.

The Culture of the Uchi

Despite the diminishing role of the family as a source of identity for its members, the culture of family is a strong one whose symbols of membership persist. Within the home there is still a strong feeling of "inside" and a strong line of demarcation between the uchi and the outside. Family members are relaxed and open with each other, but seen from the outside, the uchi is intensely private. It has secrets and a language of its own that are very seldom shared with outsiders.[4] Even in a modern urban family, there is a feeling that there are special mysteries—the kafū, or "ways of our family"—and that these customs, seen as peculiar to each family, will have to be learned by each generation and by each inmarrying bride. In a traditional household, when the mother-in-law retires and passes the rice paddle to her daughter-in-law as a symbol of her household authority, the daughter-in-law is expected to have become a full member of the family and to have assimilated the ways of the house thoroughly. In fact, differences among families in such areas as community relationships, housekeeping methods, and food preparation are small, but those differences that do exist—for example, grandmother's special way of pickling radishes—are made into significant "we-they" markers. Talents, habits, and quirks belong to "our house," convey a sense of sharing and cozy privacy, and act as symbolic markers of uchi identity.

The physical territory of even the smallest apartment or home is marked off from the outside by the *genkan* (entrance hall), the place for nonintimate communications with outsiders, who do not remove their shoes and enter the house. Family rooms are also separated into those for public and private use, even though entertaining at home is infrequent. Children do not bring friends home as often as they do in other societies. Wives and husbands meet others socially in neutral public areas, such as playgrounds, shops, and restaurants and, for men, bars and coffeehouses after work.[5] Although the small physical size of the home discourages entertaining, the feeling that the home is not a public place is equally important.

The characteristics of the Japanese family that emerge most strikingly are its dependence on the outside institutions that shape the lives of fathers and children and its singular insularity and privacy. On the one hand, it is a group at the mercy of educational and occupational demands and restrictions; on the other, it maintains its supportive and nurturing functions by isolating itself from those external systems on which it depends. So, to say the least, Japanese family structure is highly adaptive, which is vital to the readjustment to Japan of Japanese families after an overseas sojourn.

The Study

This study lies outside traditional scholarship and recognized topics in several ways. First, the returnee family has only recently been recognized as an area of inquiry. Second, my approach to the family takes in several social, psychological, and cultural perspectives. Third, some broad generalizations from relatively new arenas of sociological research have been incorporated into my study. Fourth, this work integrates an understanding of group experiences in the family and at school and work that in fact shape the lives of individuals but that have usually been separately described in the literature. Finally, the treatment of a public topic demands the analysis also of its public reception, and thus this research must present an analysis of media interpretations.

I have chosen to use a detailed but limited approach, through in-depth interviews with a relatively small sample of families whose experiences cover a reasonable range of returnee environments and reactions. This, I feel, is justified by the fact that we are covering new turf. Before extensive survey research methodologies are developed to tackle any new area, an impressionistic map of the terrain must be attempted; I try here to paint a large area with a broad brush. Many cases, and types of cases, of returnees may have been ignored, and the analysis may suffer from too much generalization. Still, the goal of capturing a real moment among real families in Japanese society and putting various experiences into perspective using several lenses gives a new kind of "documentation," if not social science scholarship in the strictest sense.

This study was undertaken with the cooperation of fifty returnee families in Japan, and with other returnee employees at the fathers' place of work. The families—fathers, mothers, and children—consented to be interviewed several times each. The approach taken in the design and analysis of the study was to concentrate primarily on problems of membership and identity and to elicit from informants the effects of the overseas sojourn on their participation in meaningful groups and institutions: for fathers, the workplace; for mothers the community and their role in their children's education; and for children, their place in the group life of the school and their anxieties about the tough race for educational credentials.

The informants live in or near Tokyo, where more than 80 percent of all Japanese returnees live. Gathering a sample, first through prior personal knowledge of people in business and government agencies who had been overseas, and then through their networks, led to a surprisingly heterogeneous collection. Unlike other domestic Japanese ways of forming associations, it appears that returnees associate less on the basis of class, occupational similarity, or long-standing connection and more as fellow returnees. They have similar experiences abroad and in Japan.

The families have children who were junior-high-school age or younger overseas and after their return. I was especially keen to include children of this age group so that the spotlight would be on the compulsory education system in Japan, which ends with junior high school. The sample included both families whose children attend special readjustment schools and families who placed their children directly in ordinary schools.

To fill out the picture of the families' return, interviews were held with a range of people involved in their lives: schoolteachers, administrators, and counselors in both ordinary and readjustment schools; academic specialists on the returnee issue; and personnel managers and executives in various organizations. (Details on the sample may be found in appendix 1.)

School

For these families, as for those who have never left Japan, the preeminent concern is their children's schooling. Education is uppermost in the minds of everyone, but for returnees it presents special problems. Since an education—in good, preferably prestigious, schools—is the single most important factor in a successful life, parents and the children themselves are prepared to go all out to obtain the best possible.

There is nearly universal agreement over the best program for a child. It consists of early training at home by a dedicated mother who listens to other mothers and reads all the latest early-childhood-education information; then admission to a good kindergarden where placement in good elementary schools is assured, acceptance at a competitive "after-school cram school," and top junior high and high schools; and finally, if successful in the stiff entrance examinations, admission to a high-ranked national university. Naturally this course demands careful planning and hard work, and every stage must be accomplished in its turn. To travel abroad, to interrupt any part of the regimen, presents problems for the child and hinders the parents' full participation in planning and monitoring their child's future.

For the returning child who has studied overseas, even for a period as short as a year, the Japanese style of school life and work often requires a major adjustment. Moreover, preparation for the crucial examinations demands a type and intensity of commitment that are rarely seen elsewhere. Work done in other educational systems is not considered useful or relevant to Japanese schools or organizations. The Japanese educational system is a well-defended, conservative institution. For the individual it is a source of all-important but untranslatable credentials, and for the occupational system, it is a sifter of talent. Returning students bring not only curricular deficiencies to the Japanese school but also behavioral and social adjustment problems that are hard to overcome. But the importance of education to their futures means that these difficult adjustments are critical.

Workplace

Because of Japan's increased participation in the international economy, major Japanese companies and government ministries have undergone important shifts of emphasis. Yet these shifts have occurred without much internal structural change. One way in which the status quo has been maintained is the use of employees who have international expertise in roles that utilize their skills while insulating the successful "traditional" Japanese workplace from their influence. By compartmentalizing the internationals in special skill-defined and less prestigious work units, the company can take advantage of their special knowledge without allowing them to create a threat to the web of internal relations.

Like the traditional uchi of the family, the company sees its own modes and style as unique and in many ways resembles an intensely self-protective clique. Relationships between peers, between superiors and subordinates, all depend on the grasp and perpetuation of the uchi's requisites and, most important of all, on uninterrupted face-to-face participation. Thus international returnees, however useful they may be to the workplace, find themselves in structural, cultural, and relational isolation.

Family

I will focus the study here on three families whose lives and experiences are in different ways representative of the return for all families. The Hayashis, an academic family back from the United States with junior and senior high school children, adjusted their sense of Japaneseness in favor of a functionally smooth return. The Kajimas, an elite banking family, reassimilated after their return from Germany by working to ensure conscious control over what was to happen. The Fujimuras, affiliated with the Foreign Ministry but in a liaison position to an international organization, suffered the most dislocation and found themselves in the most marginal positions as individuals and as a family.

On their return all the families were excluded or uncomfortably marked to varying degrees. The mother mostly bore the burden of the others, sometimes empathically and sometimes directly. That burden stems from the mother's role as a representative of family readjustment in the community—one in which she will be carefully watched by kin, neighbors, and others. Since her status and feeling of worth are primarily determined by her children's success in school, she will often feel their problems more keenly than they do themselves.

As we will learn, it is the mother whose concern for her children dominates the predeparture planning and anxiety in a family about to leave Japan for the first time. First, however, we should examine the wider historical picture of return. We will learn that in its attitudes the narrow island country to which these people return has not always been as narrow as it is now, though in Japan the opening and closing of the various doors to the outside world have always been closely watched.

2

Families and Fortunes: The History of a Cultural Paradox

The movement of people across boundaries is often accompanied by political, religious, or economic rituals—passport stamping, purification rites, or money changing. In the case of Japanese employees and their families going overseas, leaving and returning to Japan is also a most important and problem-filled *social* act. While they are Japan's most valuable people in the competitive international economy, they also face great problems as stigmatized, devalued individuals who are seen as culturally contaminated by their acquaintance with foreign ways. And, as employees, they are regarded as outside the mainstream and the upward track. The ironies in this situation are many, especially as Japan's international profile heightens, for those who raise that profile must also—sometimes with little or no success—adjust their lives and those of their families to reduce their own visibility as "foreignized" Japanese.

While the fathers' career paths are at risk, their families suffer in other realms. The women who accompany these workers overseas as wives and mothers face critical scrutiny on their return to Japan as they are measured by family and community for retaining "purity." And the children, too, are perceived as foreigners in need of "reprocessing" in special schools and classes established for them.

The exclusion, I suggest, is based in both the functional and symbolic needs of a Japanese group. The person who has lived and worked or studied outside Japan may indeed have acquired some dysfunctional "foreign" ways or forgotten Japanese habits and knowledge crucial to his or her integration in a group that demands a very precise and exacting socialization. However, because the force of the exclusion

13

these people experience in Japan is so great, it requires other explanations than purely functional ones. Even a very young child returnee
whose language and schooling are completely unimpaired will be
called "foreigner," and the least behavioral or academic problem will
be attributed to his or her overseas experience, however brief. The
language of injury and disease is used to describe such children, whose
reentry is seen as a problem for the school and classmates. They symbolize the unpredictable, disordered, and non-Japanese world, and
attempts to reassimilate them stress the need to extinguish foreignness
and show no appreciation, of course, for any cosmopolitan skills they
may show.

The separation and devaluation of the returnee make up a relatively
new phenomenon, but its origins lie in cultural preferences that have
persisted for centuries. Although the striking modernity of Japan's
material culture seems at odds with the thoroughgoing insularity of its
society, as a general matter, Japan's modern economic success has
itself relied on a domestic, inward-looking structure of family and
workplace.

Behind Success: Conflict in Culture

The economic interdependence of industrialized nations is often
threatened by the internal politics of member states. When this gets
out of hand, the results are isolationism and protectionism. What happens internally varies, of course, from country to country and from
industry to industry. Much depends on a nation's history of political
and economic relationships with the outside world and—most impor-
tantly for this study—indigenous social and cultural predispositions
affecting these relationships. In Japan the case is especially interesting.

First, the Japanese have combined extreme resource dependence
with remarkable economic success. Japan's economic and political
relationships with the other industrialized nations have stabilized over
the past forty years, and Japanese industries, although almost entirely
dependent on imported raw materials, have found relatively reliable
sources for their needs. Similarly, Japanese performance in foreign
markets has been extremely profitable, based on sensitive and efficient
use of personnel in information gathering, negotiation, manufacturing,
and marketing.

The success of the Japanese economy has also been attributed to
social causes: to the internalized work ethic and to the emotional sup-

port and security the tightly ordered society provides for the individual. The coexistence in Japanese society of a high degree of international contact and a closed and a relatively conservative social order is paradoxical: The Japanese economy relies on flexible contact with the outside world, but Japanese culture demands strict preservation of the domestic identity.

The depth and severity of the paradox is keenly felt by those Japanese who work overseas, for it is they who must personally adopt conflicting identities—international and Japanese. To make matters worse, the operations that send the largest number of employees overseas tend to be the most conservative, least flexible larger companies, banks, and government ministries, whose work styles and expectations restrict the returnee greatly. Thus, the effectiveness of Japanese business and government organizations in managing complex information and trade networks flexibly and innovatively seems to be achieved at the expense of those members whose role it is to gather information and negotiate adaptively.

Past Sojourners: The History of Japan's Internationalism

The Japanese overseas traveler has not always been deeply stigmatized, but he has always been seen as a different kind of human being. In various historical periods, the sojourner has assumed different profiles, just as the demands of his workplace have changed, affecting the status of his return to Japan.

In 1868, at the beginning of the Meiji period, the "window on the West" was only a very small peephole. Between 1859 and 1872, five hundred Japanese traveled to the United States for study, and several hundred more went to Europe. Those who went overseas were either elite students who enrolled in foreign universities or government officials on special missions to observe and learn from more advanced nations. While the number of students sent abroad was small, their missions were deemed important; one third of the Meiji educational budget was devoted to them.

This organized exposure to the outside world enabled Japanese government, industry, and academic institutions to modernize without drastic change in the patterns of behavior that governed their social and operational structure. The boundaries of Japanese society could then still be well defended by simply restricting the numbers of overseas sojourners. Other forms of control were unnecessary. Although personally affected by their sojourns, and distinctively "modern" on their return, the elite travelers of the Meiji period were not treated as displaced persons in Japan.[1]

More important to Japanese policymakers and intellectuals at this time were concerns of national status and identity—Japan's position in the wider world. Japan was regarded as technologically inferior to the West but superior in culture and social order to the rest of the industrialized world. The controversy over the path modernization should take in Japan came down to the dilemma of *wakon yosai*, or "Western technology and Japanese spirit." Meiji intellectuals were divided between those who encouraged thoroughgoing Westernization and those who gave priority to the preservation of Japanese culture.[2] The latter strongly advocated establishing a universal, national ethos. The former felt that Japan's progress was measured by its degree of Westernization and subscribed to popular Spencerian theories of the evolution of societies from primitive to advanced.

Japan's role and identity in the world were seen to depend on its rank in a Spencerian hierarchy, but there was confusion over where it stood. Was Japan part of Asia and accordingly a potential leader—the most advanced and socially coherent nation among "primitives"? Or was Japan an inferior apprentice to the West, a "younger brother" among advanced nations? By the late Meiji period, the prevailing choice was for a strong identification with the West and for "separation" from Asia. Fukuzawa Yukichi, the prominent educator and writer, stated this position strongly.

> When judgments of China and Korea are applied to our country, it hurts our foreign policy. We do not have time to wait for neighboring countries to develop and then join them in the revival of Asia. We ought instead to get away from them and join the company of Western, civilized nations. . . . If we keep bad company, we will only get a bad name.[3]

The eager discipleship and openness of the late Meiji and Taisho periods was replaced in the 1930s by the atavistic *kokutai* ideology found throughout Japanese society in xenophobic suspicion and assiduous searching for the roots—historical, mythological, and literary—of a national "Japanism."[4] It became harder to travel internationally, and it grew more difficult for imported technological, ideological, or social innovations to gain official acceptance. During the war, of course, the windows on the world were closed and shuttered; few Japanese lived overseas except as soldiers and colonizers. In this period only a few independent schools taught foreign languages, not to speak of the culture and history of the West. In wartime, Japanese cultural boundaries became as well defended as its geographical borders.

Japan's postwar years can be divided into three periods characterized by different attitudes toward internationalization: economic recovery and growth during the period 1952–64, the boom years from 1964 to the oil *shokku* of 1974, and the post-energy-crisis period of 1974 to the present.

The Occupation and recovery period for Japan represented a kind of "second opening," when Japan began new relationships with the rest of the world. Special trade and defense relationships with the United States gave Japan advantages for development. New jobs opened up in American military and civilian organizations, and many young people felt that the path to personal success lay in such work. Many went to the United States for work or education. Encouraged by a period of economic boom, by the mid-1960s, Japanese society seemed relatively open to innovation and diversity. This spirit was embodied in the upbeat international mood of the 1964 Tokyo Olympics. A visitor to Tokyo in 1964 could feel almost palpable optimism and eagerness: The new subway lines, new hotels, and dozens of English schools demonstrated Japan's desire to put its best foot forward as it emerged into the international arena.

Meanwhile, those with international skills were sought by companies and government ministries to aid in expansion, information gathering, and liaison tasks and became specialists in such communications skills. By the early 1970s, however, those who had taken advantage of the openness of the early 1960s to take up nontraditional or even foreign work began to find that their choice produced more problems than benefits. They often discovered, in fact, that affiliation with a foreign organization meant low status or even a kind of internal exile from Japanese society.[5] The ideal government and industry employee was not an innovative and aggressive leader but a safely conservative, domestic-based, team worker. And yet, just as this conservative, domestic mood began to dominate, the need for overseas work boomed. The numbers of Japanese employed overseas tripled during the period 1968 to 1975 (from 130,000 to approximately 450,000), and with this increase came a new anxiety over the effect of overseas life and work on the sojourners and the impact that large numbers of them would have on the home country.[6]

In the mid-1970s, large Japanese organizations were accurately characterized as "uniform societies."[7] Homogeneity was explicitly valued, and—at least in these large organizations—conformity had become more important than innovation. Accordingly, overseas employees tried to identify themselves with their companies in Japan rather than with the overseas locals. Too great an ability in local languages and too much personal involvement in local affairs became suspect. Distinctions in terms of advancement, home leaves, and other perquisites were made, to the advantage of those who were elite (domestic-focused) internationals and to the disadvantage of those with communications skills who acted as translators or performed liaison services. In general, the boundaries that characterized Japanese organizations were more sharply drawn, marking or excluding those whose personal histories, skills, interests, or work styles made them insufficiently Japanese.

The energy crisis of 1974 intensified Japanese ambivalence over internationalism. The worldwide problem was felt most strongly in Japan, where 86 percent of energy needs are met by imported fuels.[8] What happened was that Japanese resource dependence became a key issue at a time when the country's economic profile was at a new high. Companies began to put more money into research and development, to seek diversified sources for raw materials, and to economize through greater efficiency. While better planning research and a wider spread of suppliers have improved Japan's energy resource picture, the recession that hit Japan after the oil shokku may permanently have changed the patterns of business structure and employment. For the first time since the war, employees were laid off, smaller companies or subcontractors under the umbrellas of large industries were allowed to go bankrupt, and some retiring workers, contrary to usual practices, were not offered postretirement jobs. The energy crisis further reinforced the conservative trends that had surfaced in the late 1960s, and those trends continue to color the experiences of an increasing number of internationalized Japanese.

On the Way Out: Families Before Departure

Even before they are internationalized, many Japanese families prepare for the worst. Before going overseas, mothers, fathers, and children are subject to much advice and great anxiety. What follows is an account of one family's predeparture experience.

The Ishidas have two children, a girl of ten and a boy of six. They live in an apartment in a company housing project in Tokyo. The size of their apartment is often referred to as 2DLK: two rooms plus a dining-living-kitchen area. The main living area is a room that contains a kitchen and a small dining space and, on the other side, a Western-style sofa and armchair grouped around a television set. There are two tatami-matted rooms. In one, where the parents sleep, a low table that stands in the center of the room by day is placed to one side at night when the futon (bedding) are spread. This is the closest thing the Ishidas have to a "traditional" room, though it has little of traditional Japanese serenity because it is cluttered and the corners are piled high with books and boxes. The other separate space is the children's room, where a carpet has been laid over the tatami to protect it from the furniture and provide a little soundproofing. There are two desks on opposite ends of Western-style bunk beds, and two bookshelves. The bath, a small, modern version of the old wooden *ofuro* (a deep, narrow tub for soaking) is in a small room down a narrow hall from the toilet room. In the alcove of the lavatory is a small washing machine. Mrs. Ishida hangs out the clothes on a clothesline on the tiny balcony, and lack of space there means she must wash almost daily. In good weather she also hangs out the futon to air before folding them and putting them in the closets.

When the children were small, since they made so much noise and mess, the apartment seemed even more crowded than it was. Now that they are both in primary school, Mrs. Ishida enjoys the quiet of their time away at school and their studying at home, though she has new PTA responsibilities and must herself study their homework and quiz them frequently. She goes out to lunch only occasionally with former classmates. In the past year she has also begun to attend a tea ceremony class in the home of an older woman in the neighborhood, something she hasn't done since her high school days. Some of her friends are beginning English and French classes, and she is considering joining them. These are interesting, sociable pursuits, but she expects to have to give them up when the children are studying for exams, since she will be needed at home much more then.

Mrs. Ishida, now age 35, fills her days with the work of the home and the care of her children. She has a well-established routine of cleaning, washing, shopping, and cooking. She can have the clothes on the line in a half hour, and she has a refrigerator, stove, electric rice cooker, and other time-saving appliances. However, although she could finish her chores in two hours, she prefers to space them evenly and intersperse them with entertainment (TV soap operas, cooking shows, and housewives' exercise programs) and errands. When the children were smaller, she shopped twice a day, as much for recreation as by necessity. Since she began the tea ceremony lessons and attends PTA committee meetings, she has been shopping only once a day, but she actually prefers her earlier patterns. It is she who knows and enjoys the neighborhood, not her husband; it is she who hears the latest news of the area from the vegetable seller and the dry cleaner's assistant. She has a clean apron that she wears just for shopping, and she chooses a time before lunch or between four and five in the afternoon, when she knows that her friends will also be in the nearby shopping street. Once in a while, her husband does the shopping, but he is scarcely known by the shopkeepers or the neighbors.

When the children return from school she gives them a snack, sends her son out to play with his friends, and helps her daughter to settle down to her homework. She has had to push her a little, since she seems "slow," but she feels sorry for her and tries to make the long study hours less lonely by sitting near her or bringing her food. Mrs. Ishida is considering sending her to *juku* (after-school classes) but is concerned about the effects of competition. She also knows her daughter would not be able to pass the entrance examination for the "best" juku and worries that entering a class that some might call "remedial" would give the girl a feeling of inferiority. But she doesn't worry too much, since she feels that it is not so important for a girl to go to a top university. She is more ambitious for her son. He has a tutor once a week in arithmetic, which he seems to enjoy. A few of his classmates attend juku, but the Ishidas have decided to wait until he is eight or nine, and "tougher."

Mrs. Ishida consults with her husband on the children's progress, but he usually does not disagree with her assessments and plans. He does not attend PTA meetings nor does he help the children with their homework, though he did arrange for his son's tutor, a college student–nephew of his boss. Mr. Ishida has confidence in his wife's ability to handle their children's education, though he sometimes feels like an outsider in these decisions and is a little unhappy that he doesn't know more about his children's daily lives. But he knows more about his wife's job than she knows about his.

Mr. Ishida gets up early, between six and six-thirty, and has a quick breakfast before he runs for the bus and the two trains that take him to the office. He works for a large steel company, which he entered directly after graduating from Keio University, a prestigious private university in Tokyo. After the first two years of training and work in the home office, he was transferred to a plant on Kyushu, Japan's southernmost island. In this smaller office he learned the actual work of his company. After three years, he was sent back to Tokyo, where he married (at the age of twenty-six) and where he has lived ever since. He is now thirty-seven, and works in a specialized area of his company.

Mr. Ishida has been sent to other parts of Asia for brief stays of no more than three weeks at a time, but—unlike some of his subordinates—he has not yet been stationed abroad for longer periods. However, he has heard that the company is considering sending him to a post in the United States, and he is eager to go. Since the family would be there for about three years, his wife is less eager and worries a great deal about the children's future. These worries have caused her to have more frequent discussions with her husband, so he is currently more involved than usual in family matters, although his company hours still prevent him from having much direct contact with the children.

He works solidly through the morning, with tea or coffee at his desk, but after lunch the pace slackens. He meets friends who entered the company in the same year, his "entry mates," and chats with them in the halls. He goes to meetings and he sorts papers. There is more talk across the desks, and plans are made for the evening. When a report is due, or when the biennial reshuffle of jobs is near, people work late—hours after the secretaries have left—and send out for a noodle or "curry-rice" supper. Three or four nights a week Mr. Ishida arrives home after 10:00 P.M., and he is rarely home before 8:00 P.M. Even so, he is considered to be a family man, and he is even said to be a little too much so, since he does not often join the office gang's bar sessions.

But, however much he might like to spend time with his family, after a full day or two in the small and noisy apartment, he is happy to get out into the world again. Although he can relax at home and be well taken care of, he feels somewhat superfluous there and prefers the company of his former classmates and office mates. Thus, while the whole family likes the outings they take together on Sundays, the times when father is at home are not always relaxing. The children are told to be quiet so that he may rest. Mrs. Ishida devotes herself to her husband, making tea and snacks and watching his favorite shows.

The Ishidas discuss their future in terms of two major goals: the successful completion of their children's schooling and the purchase of a house. Although they feel an overseas posting would hurt their children's scholastic advancement, they know that the extra pay would greatly help their house fund. In spite of this, however, Mr. Ishida feels the intensity of his wife's anxiety and has promised to try to find a way

to turn the post down without harming his relationship with his superiors. Because he knows it wouldn't do to turn it down once it has
officially been offered, he is attempting, with little hope, to forestall
the delivery of the assignment. At the same time he knows that not to
look eager puts him in a bad light.

Mrs. Ishida's chief anxiety is about the children. She has talked with
her children's teachers about the prospect of several years' absence
from Japanese schools and has not been encouraged. The daughter's
teacher said that she would fall at least a year behind her classmates
and suggested that she be left with her grandmother in Japan. Since
the son is younger and is doing well in first grade, his teacher simply
suggested the use of overseas Japanese classes, correspondence
courses, and perhaps a period in a readjustment school on their return.
She said that the real problem with an overseas experience was that
the children would "get out of the habits" of Japanese education.
Although Mrs. Ishida doesn't think she suffers from *Todaibyo* (Tokyo
University sickness)—a feverish eagerness to enter a child in Tokyo
University—she believes that her feeling of responsibility for her son's
future will intensify if she goes overseas. Since any slip in his grades
would be blamed on her lack of vigilance, she would have to become
a full-time "education mama." She would have to manage both the
children's overseas local education and keep them going in Japanese
language and learning habits. The correspondence courses involve the
mother as coach, and each packet comes with a manual for her use.
Before departure the Foundation for the Education of Children Overseas will prepare her for this and other tasks in several counseling
sessions.

When Mrs. Ishida brought up the matter with friends at lunch, they
expressed great sympathy for her plight and encouraged her to stay in
Japan with the children while her husband lived abroad. However, one
of her friends, who had lived overseas for a year, took her aside later
and in a conspiratorial whisper told her that in fact she had had a won-
derful time but did not like to talk about it in Japan. Mrs. Ishida isn't
particularly consoled: One year isn't three to five years, which to her
seem like an eternity.

Although he tries to sympathize with his wife, Mr. Ishida is interested in going. Since he feels a little offtrack in any case as a specialist,
and since he isn't one of the regulars in the top promotion group, he
doesn't have a high management post at risk. He feels that he will have
a better chance to use his skills overseas than in Japan. He also hopes
that his children can enjoy a respite from the rigorous educational sys-

tem. He has bought them a large atlas and travel books about the United States, hoping both to prepare them for the trip and to interest them in learning about other countries. He is more worried about his wife, for he has heard stories of Japanese women overseas who become "neurotic" from the strain and isolation. Her school English will be little use to her, and the children will quickly leave her behind. Therefore, while he wants an American life for the children, he has resolved to find housing near other Japanese, for his wife's sake.

Mrs. Ishida has a well-ordered life. The apartment is small but manageable, and because there are only a few hours per day when everyone is home, it rarely feels cramped. As we have seen, the human relations of the household revolve around the nurturance Mrs. Ishida provides the children on the one hand and her husband on the other. She is scarcely passive in her domestic sphere, within which she makes plans and decisions. She must at times be aggressive on behalf of the children's education and a good economist on behalf of the family. Thus, her skills center on the ability to manage relationships and to develop and maintain long-range plans. As they do in her husband's firm, the efficiency and success of the home depend on a high degree of predictability of event and behavior, and as long as authority and control remain hers[9] and external circumstances pose no problem, Mrs. Ishida feels confident of success.

Mrs. Ishida's anxieties about the children's overseas education focus particularly on the fear that her own capacity to have an effect on their well-being and progress will be limited. She will not be able to help them in their local school's homework and will not be able to consult with Japanese teachers and friends. Further, she will be unable to judge her children's abilities against those of her friends' children and will, in general, lack a community of friends and neighbors. If her children learn foreign ways and speak a new language, she wonders if she will be able to maintain her relationship with her children and the control and predictability of the home.

The Ishidas did go overseas. Mr. Ishida knew that a hint is usually a precursor to an announcement and that he would not easily be able to turn down the position when it came—nor, as we've seen, did he really want to. They lived in Chicago for most of their sojourn, but the last year of their tour was spent in Atlanta.

The Ishidas' soul-searching and their attempt to develop preventive strategies to ward off the problems of their overseas sojourn manifest the desire to maintain not just their Japaneseness but the structure and function of the uchi itself. The family's reaction to the problem of overseas experiences typifies all uchis in Japan and is, of course, the reality of the domestic core of Japan.

I will go on to provide examples of several families' responses to the overseas experience and their return to Japan. We will see these families struggle to come back to school, workplace, and community. The issues involved and the outcomes vary, but all the families have conscious and sensitive perceptions of the facts of displacement.

3

Return to Japan: Three Case Histories

Coming Home: The Yappari Factor

A best-selling novel of the 1970s, serialized on Japanese television, featured a trading company executive and his family on their return to Japan.[1] The opening scene introduces us to the two children of this family, who have forgotten much of their Japanese. They feel they must protect themselves from embarrassment by guarding their faces—one with a sanitary gauze mask over her mouth and nose and the other with a motorcycle helmet—so that no one will try to speak to them. Later we are shown a humiliating scene at a school for returning children, where the mother is forced to declare herself "irresponsible" in not having provided a Japanese education for her children overseas. The problems of educating the children lead to a situation in which the family must be split up: The father is sent to a "sidetracked" post in Kyoto, and the wife and children are left in Tokyo so that the daughter may attend a readjustment school. The novel may seem overdrawn and excessively dramatic, but the many real-world stories of social ostracism and institutional compartmentalization among returnee families make it less than completely far fetched.

In any case the returning employee and his* family do encounter an unsettling ambivalence in many settings: Teachers and classmates are unsure how to treat a returnee child, and the community is usually suspicious of a returnee housewife. Employees are often greeted on

---

*For the sake of simplicity, the pronouns *he*, *his*, and *him* will be used to refer to the general case of the returnee employee. In the sample drawn for this study, almost all employees were, in fact, male.

their return (after an average of three to five years overseas) by a feeling of distance from their Japanese community greater than anything they had experienced in their physical removal—a sense of distance created by a separate track for returnees or by the negative reactions of colleagues and superiors.

Although relationships with individuals may be awkward or painful, what makes the returnee clearly offtrack in Japan is his segregation into international divisions at the firm and the segregation of his children into special classes in school. A returnee finds a workplace characterized by social homogeneity and predictability. Exposure to different styles of life and work makes a person suspect, because there is a strong group need for his behavior to conform completely to that of workmates. This homogeneity creates tests of a member's fitness. Those who fail them may be rejected or isolated. But it is not errant behavior or an atypical style of work for which a returnee is penalized as much as the *fact of his absence*. The overseas sojourn, however necessary to the work of the firm, isolates and labels the employee as different in several ways. He is functionally isolated by his international specialty, branded as potentially disruptive or aberrant, and, most important, he has been absent from the group. That very absence—from daily, face-to-face interaction—seems to present the greatest obstacle to a returnee's acceptance and integration.

This situation can be characterized by what I call the returnee's "yappari problem": *Yappari*, a word that appears in common discourse with great frequency, means roughly, "after all," "nonetheless," or "as predicted." What is most important is a person's predictability, and to be predictable means to exercise only the narrowest of options for choice, to hew to the given norm. The conservative society to which the Japanese returnee returns has no comfortable yappari understanding of his life and ways; thus, the only role he fills is that of the unpredictable other. The avoidance response of superiors and colleagues, schoolmates and neighborhoods, and the increase in institutionalized isolation, reflects a protective yappari insularity that is at odds with Japan's growing international economic involvement.

Media attention to the problems of returnees currently features children. The number of school-age children (6–15 years) returning to Japan each year has risen from 2,000 in the late 1960s to over 10,000 in 1985. Although the figure is only a very small percentage of the school population, the public attention given these children is great. Why? First, in a homogeneous and carefully calibrated educational system absence and differentness are glaringly apparent. And second, there is a sense of disjuncture between the elite status of many of the parents and the damage done to their children.

It is also easier for the media and social critics to fasten on the educational system, always open to public scrutiny, than to confront the political and business structures that carry the laurels for Japan's success. Thus, occupational maladjustment among returnees has not received as much public acknowledgment as the educational problems of returnee children. In any case, individual returnees who have left their jobs for international work, personnel managers who are in quandaries over the placement of returnees, teachers who know the problems of their students' families, and interested journalists all agree that the outcome for many who leave Japan is isolation, exile, and diminished prospects. In the media, students who have been overseas are characterized as "international masterless samurai," "wounded children," "half-Japanese," or even "foreign Japanese." There is also an interesting term, a spin-off from the returnee media attention, "inside-outsider" *(uchi no gaijin)*, meaning any kind of person who is different and who must yet be acknowledged as Japanese.

Case Histories

The Ishida family, on the verge of departure from Japan, is representative. While diversity of course exists among families who have never left Japan, much more diversity is introduced by the overseas sojourn. Returnee families are distinguished by how long they were overseas, where and when they went, by the ages and sexes of their children, and by the occupation of the father. Although the three case histories here represent three types of reentry, they by no means take in all the possible permutations. The descriptions of the three families are drawn from the sample, though the names and a few circumstances have been changed to protect their anonymity.

In all the families, we find mothers, fathers, and children who must struggle with threats of spoiled identity, damaged career paths, and, most important of all, educational prospects now greatly at risk.

The Hayashis

The Hayashi family is typical of academic families who have had short sojourns overseas. Professor Hayashi received his Ph.D. in the United

States in the 1950s and has returned twice with his family. Professor Hayashi's wife, Kumiko, has an M.A. in English literature from an international university in Tokyo and earlier spent a term in the United States as an American Field Service (AFS) student during high school. The first family sojourn occurred when their son Yukio was two years old. Their daughter Eriko was born in the United States at the end of their one-year stay. The second time away was to Boston for two years, long for an academic, but the research project with which he was connected made it necessary. During this period Kumiko worked as a part-time teacher of Japanese at a university. Yukio was fifteen and Eriko was thirteen when they returned to Japan.

The parents remember their overseas stay as a golden time for the whole family. Kumiko felt she could work without anxiety for the children and made many friends. She said she often thought of what she would be returning to in Japan, a life constrained by responsibilities and custom, and this led her to pursue an American life-style vigorously. While she was indeed worried about her children's education, she did not feel that she had to commit herself totally to them in the American schools, something she would have done in Japan. In any case, she did not understand their lessons very well. While she initially made a point of being home when the children arrived from school, she didn't object when they spent the rest of their afternoons with their friends instead of books.

Kumiko and her husband took several brief trips together, leaving the children with American neighbors, something she would never have done in Japan. Although she was, because of her job, somewhat involved with the local Japanese community, she avoided its exclusivity. The family traveled extensively in America and Canada on what the father calls "social studies trips" to teach the children about North America. In their Tokyo apartment the Hayashis have mounted a large road map of the United States with all their excursions routed— 11,000 miles' worth.

The children were less eager to leave for a second stay abroad. Having made elaborate plans to stay in Japan with an uncle, Yukio had to be bribed with the promise of a ten-speed bicycle to make him go peacefully. Moreover, the parents had to fight their children's teachers and school principals, who warned them against taking their children out of middle school. The parents took many textbooks and workbooks with them and planned to send the children to a Saturday Japanese language school in the United States. However, for most of their stay, they ignored Japanese school subjects. Until three months before their return to Japan, the Hayashis spent time teaching their children as much as they could about the United States. Just before returning, however, Mrs. Hayashi enrolled the children in Saturday language classes and began drilling them in Japanese, although her husband told her not to bother. The parents always spoke Japanese at home, but by the end of the first year, the children were replying to them and speaking to each other in English. Professor Hayashi felt that the children would be able to handle reentry and that anxiety was unnecessary. He felt that Japanese children in general were overprotected and said, *Kuro saseta hō ga ii*, "It's better for them to suffer." Mrs. Hayashi was not convinced and found herself consulting Japanese women friends more than her husband on these matters.

After returning to Japan in the fall, Eriko was enrolled in a private middle school with an international section for returnees, and Yukio entered the high school returnee class in the same school, with the expectation that he would be able to switch to a public school in April, when the Japanese school year begins. Yukio's teachers doubted that he would be able to do as he planned, for the March high school exams rarely admit late entrants. His parents also tried to prepare him for exams to a so-called "escalator" high school that feeds directly into a good private university. Kumiko worked with her son toward this end, and they hired an after-school tutor as well. She had been intending to take a teaching job at a women's junior college, but even though they needed the money, she has put the idea off for a year until Yukio is settled in school. She stays up late at night reading and says her neighbors think she is helping her son study, but she says she is actually (somewhat secretively) trying to keep up with the literary criticism important for her own career. She has had to curb her ambitions, for she had hoped to work full-time (unusual for mothers) and develop a career.

The Hayashis feel that their overseas stay was an important time for them as a family and gave them a closeness they believe Japanese families now rarely have. The parents had more time for the children, who also had more time for family activities than they do in Japan. Immediately after their return, both parents had severe reactions to being back in Japan. Professor Hayashi was quickly plunged into administrative duties at his university, which he suggests were disproportionately assigned to him by superiors and colleagues who feel he has "had his fun and now must work hard." Out of a sense of obligation and a desire to be accepted again, he has thrown himself into these tasks. He is disgusted with his lack of freedom, however, and with the elaborate relationships he must relearn to manipulate.

Mrs. Hayashi, too, feels there is no joy in Japan for her: She returns to a difficult relationship with her mother-in-law and to jealousy among her former colleagues as well as to a thwarting of her new ambitions. She sees Japan as crowded and polluted and the Japanese as overworked and narrow-minded. She now has few friends she sees regularly, except for a woman whom she met overseas. She says she would like to meet other women outside the circle of mothers at her children's school, but at the moment she has no time. She feels she has had two lives—one a relaxed American-style life and the other a self-conscious Japanese life.

The Kajimas

The Kajimas, who lived for five years in Düsseldorf, West Germany, had a very different experience. Mr. Kajima works for a large bank that has long had a branch in Germany. There are ten Japanese employees in the German office and they are part of a large Japanese community in Düsseldorf.[2] Mr. Kajima's elite status allows him to do some international business without affecting his position. That status is based in part on family background, which includes an uncle who is a former vice-minister of finance, and his father, who is president of a medium-size manufacturing company. But more than pedigree, the prestige of his university degree and the understanding that he himself had to work hard to get there give him credibility. Like his father and uncle, he is a graduate of the law division of Tokyo University.

His wife, a graduate of Tsuda Women's University, is the daughter of a retired Tokyo University professor. She may be best described by the American phrase "a real lady"—well educated, with proper manners and a sense of confidence in her position.

The Kajimas have three children. At the time of their return to Japan, their daughter Sumiko was thirteen, and their two sons Yoshi and Kazuo were eight and six respectively. Throughout their stay in Düsseldorf, the children (except for the youngest) attended local schools and Japanese classes on Saturdays. Kazuo went to kindergarten in a British school.

While the children mixed easily with local children and (except for the youngest) spoke German well, the parents had few intimate contacts with German families. Mr. Kajima says that "bankers are like that" and rarely mix, but Mrs. Kajima blames the Germans for being "too private," for excluding them. Mr. Kajima was surprised that the international business community seemed aloof and felt that the lack of respect he experienced was because Germany—like Japan—is a seniority-based society. Hence, "We Japanese always look younger than we are to them, and they also don't know that we are of high status in Japan." Mrs. Kajima also suspects part of the problem stems from European racism. Yet she made no strong attempts to meet German women by joining clubs or classes (except for agreeing to teach a flower-arranging class). Instead, she belonged to a group of Japanese women who took German lessons together, toured museums, and went to concerts. None of the family especially liked German food, which they said was too greasy and heavy, but they nonetheless loved the sausages. Meanwhile, Mr. Kajima became proficient in distinguishing regional beers and ales. Mrs. Kajima tried to provide "healthier Japanese meals" but had to make compromises. The Kajimas entertained Japanese and a few Americans and traveled throughout Europe.

Their return to Japan was carefully planned. Mrs. Kajima contacted a cousin who has a child in an "escalator" school for a good women's university, and she helped arrange for Sumiko to be admitted there. Since Yoshi and Kazuo were tested to be near grade level in math and Japanese, they enrolled them directly in public schools. Mrs. Kajima flew home with the children ahead of her husband so that the children could enter schools in April, according to the Japanese schedule. Sumiko was disconsolate and quite emotional about leaving her friends in Germany, and she writes to them often. Just after their return the two boys kept asking, "When are we going home to Germany?" But the Kajimas do not worry about them, and the children have shown no signs of readjustment problems, such as psychosomatic symptoms or refusal to do schoolwork or speak Japanese.

Mr. Kajima had little worry that his career would be damaged by his stay overseas, but to make sure, he traveled to Japan at least once a year to check in at the home office and to appear at important meetings. Mr. Kajima is clearly conscious of having been away, but says many others have more trouble than he does, partly because he maintained communications carefully. He says his background and work make him a mainstream insider and that the domestic focus in his career ironically makes him free to be more international. As he said, however, not everyone is encouraged and supported in making these "home stops," and it may be that his superiors were ensuring his ultimate safe passage home—that he wasn't *destined* to be an outsider. Other men in his section who have lived overseas are used as translators, asked to be hosts to foreign visitors, or are relegated to international liaison work, and it is this kind of international that Mr.

Kajima has carefully avoided becoming. Even now he avoids talking about his own experience in Germany and instead cultivates a generalized savoir faire about the world at large.

Mrs. Kajima has much free time in Japan. She has a part-time household helper—her mother's maid who works for her two days a week. So Mrs. Kajima practices her hobby of flower arranging and sees her friends. Her life in Japan is not very different from her life in Germany, but she, like her husband, knows that she should not speak of Germany too often and says her friends would be jealous if she did. She is afraid that they might exclude her as they did other women who, after returning from the United States, seemed to them to be flaunting their differentness. Mrs. Kajima has put away her German fur coat and wears only clothes bought in Japan.

The Fujimuras

The third family, the Fujimuras, represent in part what the Kajimas can avoid: alienation and sidetracking or, in the case of the husband's occupation, becoming what might be called an international dropout. Mr. Fujimura works in the Foreign Ministry as a liaison with an international organization. This affiliation is interesting to him and gives him diverse tasks, but he is treated as a kind of glorified translator.

The Fujimuras lived in the United States for three years with their son Yasu, who was ten years old on his return to Japan. Mr. Fujimura is a graduate of Kyoto University and his wife, of a Christian university in Tokyo. Her parents are devout Christians—her grandfather worked for an American missionary in Japan in the 1920s. She herself is not a practicing Christian, but she says her background provided her with a broader idealism that sustains her in difficult times. Mr. Fujimura's father was a manufacturer who wanted his son to take over the company. When the younger Fujimura was a teenager, however, he contracted a debilitating kidney ailment and was bedridden for over a year. During this time he read and thought a lot about his future, and he says he experienced a kind of conversion. He decided to try to go to a foreign university, but he could not because of his illness and his parents' objections. Unlike many of his classmates, he worked hard at Kyoto University and passed a middle-grade ministry examination. His professor helped him choose a position for the opportunities it would offer in international work. After five years in the ministry, he requested and received an assignment in Paris, and after two years there, he returned to Japan, married, and hoped to settle in Tokyo. However, he was again sent to Europe, this time to Prague, for a year. His wife was pregnant and stayed in Japan. When Yasu was six, they were sent abroad again, this time to the United States.

The child's future was their primary concern, since Mr. Fujimura had become disillusioned about his life as an international in the ministry. He wanted to do everything he could to keep his son out of a compartmentalized career. So, before leaving Japan, he and his wife went to the counseling service provided by a foundation* to plan a strategy. Since he was used to giving advice to mothers only, the counselor was a little uneasy talking to both husband and wife. He accordingly directed his attention to Mrs. Fujimura as the responsible parent. He recommended that she attend the predeparture orientation lectures for wives and that they enroll the child in the foundation's correspondence course and in a Japanese school in the United States. Later, in the booklets furnished by Japan Airlines' Family Service,[3] the Fujimuras read about medical preparation for overseas life, including long lists of diseases the child might get, information about foreign medicine, and care of teeth and eyes under "dangerous overseas conditions." In the area of emotional preparation, they were exhorted to help their child overcome inferiority feelings that might develop out of being an outsider with no knowledge of the local language. Finally, they were advised to decorate the child's room with Japanese ideographs and pictures to remind him of Japan.

Once overseas, based in Washington, D.C., Mr. Fujimura enjoyed the challenge of his work and Mrs. Fujimura enjoyed new hobbies— learning to weave and do needlepoint—and meeting women in the neighborhood. They lived in a bedroom suburb in Maryland. Mrs. Fujimura took English lessons at a small community college and met a wide range of women and retired men from many countries. The local church became a focal point of her life, and she felt comfortable in a women's group there that arranged outings and parties for the children, and classes for the mothers. Yasu was quickly assimilated into his grammar school class, which was very diverse in its makeup. While at first it seemed to the Fujimuras that there were no standards at all, it became clear that these children really were more tolerant, "looser," and accepting than those in Japan, and cultural and behavioral differences became a rationale for rather than an obstacle to a sense of community. At least, this is how Mr. Fujimura likes to explain

---

*See Chapter 4.

it. The Fujimuras forgot the warnings of the foundation and allowed their son's Japanese lessons to lapse.

When they returned to Japan, the Fujimuras worried about their son, who they felt was rather "wild" though very bright, and who resisted adapting to Japanese school customs. He was in a readjustment class for three months at the Family School,[4] where, as he says, he just "fooled around." Mr. Fujimura's ministry helped pay Yasu's tuition there through its personnel division. Now Yasu is in the fifth grade at a public school in their neighborhood, in the eastern part of Tokyo. He is the only returnee in his class and is treated gently by the teacher, who makes excuses for him when he misbehaves on the grounds that he has been overseas and cannot know any better. His classmates at first regarded him as a curiosity and called him *gaijin* (foreigner). He seems to have decided that a good offense is the best defense and behaves very aggressively as the leader of a group of "tough guys."

Mr. Fujimura went into a mild depression after returning to Japan, accompanied by weeks of poor appetite, insomnia, and headaches. He expresses much dissatisfaction at life in Japan, but feels that they must live in Japan at least until their son has finished his education, because "there is no other life for a Japanese." At least he does not want to sacrifice his son because of his *own* discomfort in Japan. He has found comfort in a few old college friends and in an old and very Japanese pastime that his father enjoyed, the tea ceremony. He now describes himself as a romantic melancholic.

His wife has decorated their living room with her weaving and needlepoint and seems happy to be home in Japan, saying, *sumeba miyoko*, "Wherever we are, it's home." She spends much of her free time at her mother's house. She is not especially interested in meeting other returnees, in seeking out foreign women as friends, or even in reestablishing relationships with her former Japanese friends. The family seems to exist in a kind of limbo, a time of waiting, between life overseas and life in Japan.

Family Attitudes

These families have one very important thing in common: their children's dependence on a Japanese education. Although other elements of their lives may diverge, it is this factor that makes immediate and—in some instances—frightening demands on all of them. However "internationalized" they might have become, none of the parents is willing to sacrifice the future of his or her child in Japan to new ideals or life-styles. All of them were worried—before, during, and after an overseas sojourn—about the effect it would have on the children. Second is concern about the father's career. The fathers invested substantial energies in attempts to ensure smooth returns to the home office. As for family life, all felt greatly rewarded by "togetherness" overseas, and difficult adjustments had to be made back to a Japanese family pattern.

The Hayashis, the Kajimas, and the Fujimuras represent three patterns of reentry. All shared characteristic concerns but exhibited variations in type as they tried to reassimilate into Japanese society. Having adopted a Western perspective on family life, the Hayashis now feel that Japanese society is restrictive, hectic, and unsupportive of family unity. However, because they are also practical and determined, the Hayashis do not feel victimized and feel a certain amount of control over their lives.

The Kajimas orchestrated their return well. They reassimilated, but with an insider's canniness and assurance rather than panic or paranoia. Mr. Kajima knew the ropes, and with his connections he was able to readjust without friction. There was little real danger for him, and his confidence has extended to the family's handling of the children's return.

The Fujimuras, however, based their internationalism on abstractions and idealism. Being nonmainstream was a fact of life for them; this kept them from paying attention to the details of occupational and educational reentry that would have smoothed their path. Although they went about doing all the "correct" things, such as consulting with counselors, they enjoyed overseas life too much to maintain the recommended regimen. The family's enthusiasm for American life was perhaps based on Mr. Fujimura's early feelings of being an outsider in Japanese society and on Mrs. Fujimura's Christian training—both of which gave them an abstract and sentimental attachment to the West and prevented them from having a balanced view of either American or Japanese society. The situation seemed black and white to them: They had either to be "pure" Japanese insiders or totally alienated internationals. They saw every sign of their differentness as a permanent stigma and responded to pressures to conform with depression and retreat.

Meanwhile, though all the parents agreed that the Japanese school system presented a big problem, and all felt that Japanese society cannot easily assimilate differentness, the three families can nonetheless be characterized by different "tones" of negativism about Japan: the Hayashis' more distant critical stance, the Kajimas' confident sense of irony, and the Fujimuras' disappointed and somewhat sad frustration.

Family Support

Unlike other groups, institutions, and organizations in Japan, the family is the ultimate source of support. However threatened in outside groups and systems by exclusion or compartmentalization, the individual can count on the family to develop strategies that minimize the effect on him or her and on the family as a unit. In other words the family is a group that does not stigmatize a member for differentness but rather protects him or her from exposure[5] and pressures him or her to conform to outside community values to minimize strain.

This often produces some minor internal strains. Deviant behavior acquired overseas may create intrafamily problems, but these are not considered very serious. Adolescent children may chafe at the evening curfews imposed by parents in Japan or may resent the lack of privacy in a Japanese house. A young wife returning to her mother-in-law's house is rarely dismissed as incorrigibly corrupted, nor are grandchildren who may scarcely remember how to speak the language rejected. In general, the difference between the flexibility of kin relations and the rigidity of relationshps outside the family shows that family bonds are based on a diffuse kind of dependency (amae), while the workplace and school depend on predictability and conformity that discourage deviance. An employee whose language or style is seen as un-Japanese may be permanently sidetracked as "handicapped" in the outside world, but within the family such a person is for the most part patiently reeducated.

Family Problems and Benefits

Accordingly, though few problems affect the family as a whole after its return to Japan, individual experiences in outside institutions require family support. Because of automatic seniority-based pay increases, the father's earning power is rarely hurt unless he changes jobs.[6] A few families said that their inability to put their children into normal Japanese schools caused the whole family severe psychological strain. For increasing numbers of overseas Japanese, the chief problem caused by the overseas sojourn is the separation of family members. Either the mother and children stay in Japan for the term of the father's posting, or the children are boarded with relatives or in dormitories in Japan while the parents live overseas. The first is the more frequent pattern, yielding large numbers of "overseas bachelors" and fatherless households.

This often produces great strain. A young mother, for example, who came for counseling at the offices of the Foundation for the Education of Children Overseas, said that her husband had just gone to Saudi Arabia to work and was looking for a home for his family, which he expected would soon join him. He wrote to his wife, "I must frequently entertain Western businessmen and without a wife as hostess I am at a loss. I really want you to come." She was of course worried about the children's education, and wrote back saying she would not come. The counselor told her to go since it is better to keep the family together, and advised her to enroll the children in overseas Japanese classes in Saudi Arabia. She angrily replied that if her children suffered, she would hold the counselor responsible. But after several more hours of discussion, she was persuaded to go.

Some families decide to leave their children in Japan. (See Table 1.) In 1976 it was reported that 3,705 children remained in Japan while their parents lived overseas for two to five years. The number represented 19 percent of the school-age children of parents assigned overseas. Forty-nine percent of the students who stay behind are in elementary school, 27 percent in middle school, and 24 percent in high school. However, given the total number of children in overseas families, elementary school students who are left in Japan are only 13 percent of the total, middle-school students are 28 percent, and high school students are 49 percent. This clearly shows that tensions and fears about education intensify as children become older. Larger absolute numbers of younger children are left in Japan because overseas families are young (with an average parental age of thirty-six). Similarly, there are fewer families with children of high school age because the parents in such instances are older. As might be predicted, the families that leave their children behind are most often stationed in developing countries, which can be seen in Table 2. The same report shows that of all the children who do not accompany a parent on overseas assignment, 84.2 percent are in a parent's care, usually the mother's, and only 15.8 percent are in the care of someone else. Ninety-three percent of the left-behind children live in relatives' homes, 2.6

TABLE 1

JAPANESE CHILDREN OF OVERSEAS FAMILIES
BY TYPE OF SCHOOL, 1976

	Total	Elementary		Total	Middle	High
		Lower	Upper			
Children left behind	3,705	877	932	1,809	1,012	864
(Percentage)	100.0	23.7	25.2	48.8	27.3	23.9
Children accompanying overseas families	15,770	7,250	5,033	12,283	2,570	917
Children of families assigned overseas (total)	19,475	8,127	5,965	14,092	3,582	1,801
Left-behind children as percentage of total	19.0	10.8	15.6	12.8	28.3	49.1

TABLE 2

JAPANESE CHILDREN OF OVERSEAS PARENTS
BY COUNTRIES OF POSTING, 1976

	Totals	Developing	Advanced
Children left behind	3,692 (100%)	2,636 (71.4%)	1,056 (28.6%)
Children who went overseas	15,770	6,291	9,479
Total of children	19,462	8,927	10,535
Left-behind children as percentage of total	19.0	29.5	10.0

percent live in dormitories, and 2.4 percent live in company-owned facilities for children of employees. Japanese families usually believe—and believe strongly—that a child must be cared for by relatives. The use of boarding schools, babysitters, and other nonfamily care has never been popular.[7]

In a few cases, the family saw life overseas as almost entirely positive. In these families, women who at first found overseas life awkward soon became used to sharing the work and responsibilities with their husbands and, on their return to Japan, felt burdened or lonely when the men could no longer give much time to the family. Children remember the pleasure of long family vacations. With no juku and less homework than in Japan, they could pursue hobbies and sports and develop neighborhood friendships. Yet most of the boys who reported taking up a hobby overseas chose very Japanese hobbies: memorizing Japanese poems, paper folding (origami), and following sumo wrestling or kendo swordplay in Japanese magazines. Girls' hobbies tended to be more social and less traditional—such as piano and photography—activities that would not exclude foreign friends.

Mothers, too, had more time for their families and for themselves. And fathers relied on their families for entertainment and relaxation overseas, especially in places where the Japanese community was small. For many this was a happy time, and some families have tried to maintain their overseas togetherness in Japan. Fathers have avoided after-work drinking sessions and take work home instead of staying late at the office. Mothers have tried to entertain foreign guests at home, though this means they must swallow their embarrassment about their small, crowded living spaces. If Japanese guests are entertained, very elaborate foods must be prepared and the children dispatched to grandmother's house or somewhere else—all of which makes the women realize why so much Japanese entertaining takes place outside the home.

After their return, many children in families that feel positively about their overseas experience do not at first attend extra tutoring sessions. But the after-school playtime that they enjoyed overseas is soon converted to study time; they find no one to play with because everyone else is at after-school classes. Families persisting in their family or individualistic orientation often spawn rumors: In one case, an entire suburban community was abuzz with the story that a returnee family no longer ate rice and that they spoke to each other at home only in English. When the children were teased about this, they tried to persuade their parents to become "real Japanese."

The family as uchi, or protective and nurturing unit, serves to bridge the re-entry gap. It serves as a buffer for the tensions of return and, more actively, develops strategies to help its members readjust to the external institutions to which they belong—fathers to the workplaces, children to the schools, and mothers to the local communities.

The Women's Return

As the center of the family, the woman manages its readjustment to Japan, even though the problems that receive the most public attention exist outside the home and involve the father and children in workplace and school. The housewife generally exerts pressure on her family to conform to the norms of society—the company and school—since the measure of her success or failure is her family's acceptability in the soto world. The housewife's chief role as mother is to direct her children's scholastic progress. Because educational readjustment presents the most dramatic reentry problems, she experiences pressure of the most intense kind. Although her own readjustment to kin and community is often a problem for her, nothing looms as large as the prospect of a child's failure in the Japanese educational system.

All women in the sample attempted to reassimilate as completely as possible, since none actively wanted an offtrack education for her children, and all saw it as their job to prevent their children's permanent stigmatization. But they differed in personal goals and plans, and in the style they cultivated—either taking advantage of overseas life to make some change in their lives or assiduously reconstituting a "pure" Japanese housewife style.

All mothers agreed that the pressure and intensity of study toward the entrance exams were destructive and that they and their children both suffered. Yet no one was willing to try the *shikata ga nai* (there's no help for it) approach, and no one simply knuckled under: Everyone placed children in tutoring, in juku, or in other special classes.

All the women shared the insecurity and anxiety their husbands felt in their jobs, which led to some awkwardness in their relationships with wives of their husbands' nonreturnee colleagues. But when asked, "What was most important to you in the return to Japan?" they most often mentioned their children's education, followed by their own relationships with friends and relatives. Only when specifically asked did they talk about their husbands' readjustments.

While the general set of circumstances was the same for all women in the sample, they used a variety of adjustment strategies. The woman who thought she had to be as Japanese as possible observed a very strict checklist of personal and social traits and maintained a "perfect" Japanese home, so as not to be vulnerable to charges of differentness or neglect of family. She tried to become a women's-magazine model housewife, using all the recipes, cleaning hints, and daily routines suggested in the media. If she joined any outside group, it was a PTA committee or a class in cooking, sewing, or crafts. She aired her futon daily, prepared impeccable lunches for her children, shopped primarily in the neighborhood to maintain good relationships with shopkeepers and neighbors, and never ordered take-out foods from local restaurants for her husband's late-night suppers but made everything herself. She wore a clean apron over a Japanese-bought skirt and blouse when she shopped or when she carried garbage to the apartment-building trash area. She met her young children at the school gate daily to walk them home and sometimes even took the older ones to their juku instead of letting them travel alone.

A more moderate adjuster didn't toe the line quite so rigorously, but neither did she go out of her way to exhibit differentness. While she encouraged her children to work hard and discouraged such foreign habits as taking sandwich lunches to school, she hoped that they would retain their foreign language ability and even enrolled them in a weekend English or other language-maintenance program. She herself wanted to participate more widely in outside activities and joined English, literary, or, in some cases, political study groups that met during school hours at local community halls or cultural centers. Her husband occasionally helped with housework on the weekends, but she maintained the responsibility for the house, children and community tasks.

Finally, the most international woman asserted her difference. She defiantly wore her red slacks or other foreign-bought garb; took a part-time job; sometimes even allowed her children to let themselves into an empty house after school; and entertained with her husband. Unhappily isolated from other women, she might seek out other returnees or foreign women as friends, but she lacked the very close primary relationships of kin and school friends on which most Japanese women depend. More than others, she looked to the family to provide her with social and emotional sustenance and took up the slack with political, intellectual, or career activities. Whether she herself has decided to be international or whether the choice has been forced on her by a hypercritical community, she must cope with the attendant stigma and isolation.

Whatever her strategy, or whatever the type of identity forced on her, the housewife as the key figure in the family must be strategist for her children's futures and her husband's support and comforter—she is a one-person organization that exists as a kind of subcontractor to the educational and occupational systems, providing both with clean, healthy, and well-socialized members. Her ability to perform the role may have been diminished by the overseas sojourn, but this comes more from restrictions in the educational and occupational systems than from intolerance or lack of flexibility in the family. Her own adjustment, insofar as it is possible to separate it from that of the family, seems to depend on her attitudes toward involvement in overseas life, on her early background in Japan, on her aspirations (if any) for a professional career, and on her feelings of embeddedness in a community of friends and relatives. The ultimate test of her social value lies, however, in her ability to support her husband and children in their occupations and schools. The demands involved invariably place great strains on returnee housewives.

4

Facing the Schools: The Lessons of Readjustment

Yukio's Return

Yukio Hayashi has confronted the system. He returned to Japan when he was fifteen years old, first entering a returnee class and then a regular class. According to his parents Yukio has "recovered" from his overseas experience. Meanwhile, his teachers say he is a "normal Japanese" now and credit his parents with his successful reentry, citing the extra classes and tutoring they arranged and the emotional support they provided.

Yukio's mother especially devoted herself to her children's learning, both overseas and back in Japan. In the United States, Kumiko Hayashi interested Yukio in studying Japanese and subscribed to Japanese magazines and book clubs for him.

At the end of Yukio's first year in junior high school, the family left for the United States, full of anxiety. Yukio was unhappy from the time he found out they were leaving, in December, until the moment he set foot off the plane in Boston. He had spent three months anticipating the horrors of America: He would miss his friends and was worried because he knew almost no English. Even as his ten-year-old sister was excited about going, Yukio felt sadder and wiser, burdened with the responsibilities of his advanced age.

The family had prepared aggressively for the sojourn, enrolling both children in the Japanese Saturday school in Boston and finding the very best neighborhood and schools for the children. Kumiko also enrolled Yukio in a Japanese correspondence course and intended to work with him after school every day on his Japanese language skills, Japanese social studies, and math.

Yukio stopped worrying the minute he landed. He made new friends, and loved Boston. He was a star on the softball team, an ace in an after-school computer club, and very popular with his teachers and classmates. Although his parents were pleased with his adjustment, they worried about the possible trade-off: The more he loved Boston, the harder they felt it would be for him to throw off what he'd learned on his return to Japan.

And, in fact, it was rough on everyone when they finally returned three years later. Kumiko again mobilized herself, but with less optimism and greater difficulty, for she too had changed. What lay before her, the intense commitment to her children's education, she viewed with some dread, but she felt she had no choice but to pull out all the stops and fit in.

Yukio entered the high school returnee class in which he knew no one. He did reasonably well and switched to the regular class, but his schoolwork was uneven: His spoken Japanese was fine, though he was less able than the others to calibrate social distinctions requiring various speech forms and so wasn't always as polite or informal as circumstances demanded. His math ability was excellent, though his methods of calculation and preparation of classwork differed from his classmates'. Accordingly, his family found tutors and extra classes for him to attend. Overall, he was unhappy and frustrated and felt that no one understood what he was going through: He began to have severe stomachaches, and after six months he was diagnosed as having a preulcerous condition.

The family went into a deep panic, and both parents spent hours with counselors, doctors, and all of Yukio's teachers. What frustrated Kumiko was that his academic work was very good and yet he suffered, and she struggled to find out what was wrong.

Kumiko's checklist of adjustment factors didn't include, however, one important and mostly uncontrollable reality: the problem of *ijime*, or "bullying," in her son's school. While most incidents occurred in the third year of middle school, Yukio's reentry had touched off some sparks early. His classmates were trying to create a scapegoat, a focus, for their own anxieties about fitting in, and Yukio's readymade differentness made him a target.

Over the summer vacation Yukio attended more readjustment classes. The last two weeks, however, he went by himself to visit a cousin's family in the countryside, and there at last he genuinely relaxed. When he returned to the city, he felt strong and was ready again for school.

A boy who had become his best friend was the key for him: Even though they were both busy with schoolwork and extra study, the friend persuaded him to start a school newsletter with him, and together they began collecting news, asking teachers for advice, and enlisting other classmates to help. Almost overnight Yukio became a "regular kid" in the eyes of his classmates, and even an important one. The newsletter had a brief but popular life, for in January of their second year, it was eclipsed by the pressure of study. However, by then it had done its work and Yukio, though not quite a big man on campus, was fully instated as a good citizen. Few of his "foreign habits" remained, and he'd physically outgrown all the telltale American clothing.

Yukio's return illustrates some of the problems others have faced—problems coming from both a personal "culture shock" and less-than-smooth reintegration at school. The absence of fit sometimes becomes permanent: Returnee children may find themselves out of step with classmates, out of the running for top universities, and out of the mainstream occupational system. While Yukio's readjustment ultimately depended on his peers, the source of his problems was the structure of the educational system. We need an overview of Japanese education and its role as socializer of the young.

Education and Social Integration

Education in Japan, as in many modern societies, has three important functions: to create an educated populace, to provide credentials needed in the occupational system, and to train children in the norms and behavior of the culture. In Japan's tightly ordered and homogeneous society, it is the educational system, itself well organized and uniform, that explicitly encourages a predictability, if not a monolithic uniformity, in each generation socialized. It is this predictability that often confounds the returnee, and students like Yukio must learn quickly what is expected.

Much of the success of the modern Japanese economy can be attributed to the social training that, together with a demanding educational curriculum and very high standards, guarantees a well-educated and hardworking labor force. Japanese organizations are confident that those who have done well in the educational system will later also demonstrate an acceptable style and work habits. An agreement accordingly exists that those who lack Japanese educational credentials will *not* be appropriate to a Japanese workplace.

The mandate given the educational system to socialize young Japanese comes from a consensus across society, especially from the family and the occupational system. Once, the traditional family provided social training, but today's small, isolated modern family has a diminished capacity for the role, which has passed to the schools. Meanwhile, employers have relied on the educational system to produce appropriately trained candidates since the late nineteenth century, when education was regarded as the nation's best hope for producing the people who would help Japan become a modern nation.[1] Throughout, a centralized educational administration and uniform goals and curriculum have helped to ensure a predictable and homogeneous population.

Although at various times—the present among them—there has been great interest in educational experimentation and innovation, Japanese education in practice remains conservative and uniform. The response of the educational bureaucracy to private and public calls for change is characteristically defensive, although recent discussions of educational reform have been initiated by the prime minister and have actively engaged the Ministry of Education and the private sector.

Harmony and Struggle: Goals and Methods of Japanese Education

Education is seen by curriculum planners as both a socializer for life in Japanese society, which values harmony and cohesion, and as preparation for occupations that demand hard work and discipline. Harmony is manifested in the uniformity of educational experiences, in minimizing differences between children, and in the positive value placed on cooperation. That on a given day all third-graders in Japan are working at the same level in arithmetic, that teachers expect children to follow regular and predictable routines of classroom behavior, and that the twice-yearly sports day follows a single sequence of events throughout Japan are evidence of the uniformity encouraged by centralized planning and administration.

Recently, however, the pressures of examination competition have become at least equally compelling as the major focus of education. Because of the increased pressure surrounding selection for the best jobs in the best organizations—dependent on passing examinations for the best universities and often on earlier exams for the best high schools—preparation for these examinations dominates many children's lives.

In short, both goals—cohesion and selection—tend to foster an atmosphere of conservatism in Japanese education.

Examinations

Tests for high school and college entrance are the focus of many children's lives for at least eight years, from about the age of ten to the age of eighteen.[2] The high school entrance examinations are set by the Ministry of Education, and national university examinations are prepared by faculty under ministry guidance. The ministry also approves examinations administered by private universities.[3] Success in these extremely detailed multiple-choice examinations depends on careful and thorough study of a common core of materials. The national curriculum is assiduously followed by the teachers, parents, and tutors of the children preparing for examinations and is well supported by a consensus that the meritocratic selection system produces a well-trained population from which a certified, competent elite emerges.

The pressures of the examination system are felt by all family members, but most acutely by mothers and sons. While girls are to some degree affected, the occupational future of males especially depends on their educational credentials. Children submit to long hours of study, pampered and fussed over by their mothers, who stake their own reputations in the community and their self-worth as mothers on the outcome of the exam. There are in fact special classes for mothers to train them as coaches for their children, and mothers often subscribe to magazines and buy books that help them help their children.

This kind of care, devotion, anxiety, and protection reaches its peak at examination time, when mothers ignore everything else to bring their attention to bear exclusively on their children. For those students who must travel to Tokyo to take their examinations, arrangements are made to maintain a supportive environment. Hotels offer special "examination plans" with accommodations for high school students and their mothers. According to a newspaper account, "the price includes two meals especially designed for easy digestion, access to a trio of student counselors, a map of Tokyo showing all colleges and transportation routes, and use of a student lounge equipped with dictionaries, pencil sharpeners, hot tea and cold soft drinks."[4]

There is no maternal embarrassment over turning down invitations and ignoring PTA and other obligations during this time. Tensions raised during the examination period occasionally produce extreme reactions. Annually, at exam time, there are reports in the press such as the case of a woman who strangled a neighbor's toddler who disturbed her son's study[5] or of a father who dressed as a teenage girl to take an examination for his daughter.[6] Although their incidence is low, bullying, violence, and psychosomatic ailments are cited as products of examination pressure and conformity. In 1985, a series of nervous breakdowns during middle-school entrance exams was well publicized.[7]

Bifurcation: The Classroom and the Juku

Under conficting pressures to preserve the traditional values of cohesion and harmony while at the same time ensuring the best possible preparation for the highly competitive examinations, education in Japan has undergone an interesting bifurcation. Two types of schooling have emerged. One type is the training in the public school classroom, where the egalitarian treatment of students allows no child to be advanced or kept back. The age group stays together, sometimes at cost to the brighter children, since no one is kept back or advanced by ability, and slower children are often paired with faster to give the former a boost. Both in the values taught and in the mode of work, cohesion and nonjudgmental egalitarianism characterize the classroom. Many parents, however, see this aspect of Japanese education as peripheral to the goal of success in entrance examinations and look elsewhere for hard-edge exam training. They send their children to private coaching schools (juku) and tutors for the disciplined and competitive cramming they feel is necessary for success in the examinations.[8]

The current era has been called the *ranjuku jidai,* or "period of rampant juku," and in middle-class neighborhoods it is becoming rare to see children over eight years old at home or playing after school or on weekends. Many children between third and eleventh grades spend half their waking hours in extra classes and doing extra homework, apart from their regualr school commitments. Typically, a child comes home after school, picks up a quick snack and his juku homework, and attends juku classes for another three or even four hours. It is not uncommon to see a child dozing on a train after 9:00 P.M., returning home from juku to begin his homework. The current saying goes, "With four hours sleep you pass, with five hours you fail."

Parents regret the time, pressure, and expense the classes cost their children and themselves. On the one hand, they regret the examination system that created the need for them, but on the other, they feel that the regular schools have abdicated their responsibility for the children's future by ignoring the need for stiff competitive work. Ministry of Education officials informally agree that the ministry has dragged its feet on the issue of the toll the examinations take on the educational process. They also acknowledge that juku, by priming students for the rigors of the exams, allow the mainstream schools to continue to focus on harmony and cooperation. The ambivalence within the system over this issue has perhaps encouraged the creation of juku.

Teachers, too, regret the division of function in education. Regular teachers say they feel like baby-sitters, while juku teachers often feel like drill sergeants. Whereas a child's homeroom teacher could once speak authoritatively on the child's scholastic standing and was often consulted as a guidance counselor by parents, he or she is now usually ignorant of the child's progress in the high-pressure juku and cannot feel as involved in his future. According to the teachers, parents no longer approach them with the same respect and humility but use teachers as scapegoats for their anxieties over their children's future. Teachers also complain that those children who have been pushing ahead in juku first show off, then are bored, and sometimes present disciplinary problems. Finally, the fees that teachers used to earn through after-school tutoring of slower children are now siphoned off to the juku, and now such arrangements may even be seen as improper.[9]

In such an atmosphere it is easy to see why reform of the system—or rather, of the division of labor between the two systems—is difficult to achieve. While teachers in regular schools and the union push for more egalitarian, creative education and more emphasis on "educating the whole child"—and, incidentally, cutting the six-day school week to five days—juku instructors and parents push even harder to reduce vacation and weekend "free" time and to add more hours of homework to push children ahead of the pack.[10]

The division of function between the regular schools and the juku complicates the returnees' adjustment to the educational system as a whole. The schools demand their social conformity, and the juku insist on specialized skills they may well have forgotten or have difficulty in acquiring. They must struggle to belong and to do well in both contexts, however, since they must have educational credentials to succeed in Japanese society. While the rigidity of the system forces returnees to conform or be excluded, it must also be recognized that the differentness they represent threatens the cohesion of the educational system itself.

The Ministry of Education: Patrolling Uniformity

The Ministry of Education is responsible for the uniform content and style of Japanese education.[11] Because of the success of the system in creating a populace as well educated as any in the world, and because of the success of the organizations that employ the graduates of the system, there has been little external pressure to innovate, and the Ministry of Education itself has earned a reputation for conservatism in the content and administration of education. Moreover, the ministry itself is not regarded as a place for an elite government career, and—although it employs many extremely well-qualified and hard-working bureaucrats—it does not attract the most creative or ambitious candidates from the best universities.

An example of the general confusion and ambiguity about the meaning of an international educational experience exists within the ministry itself. Recently the issue has become a focal point for talk of change in the educational system. To some the goal of "international education" is the development of an "international mind" in children, while to others the same phrase means classes for the reprocessing of "accidentally internationalized" children. To Japanese government and business leaders and educational reformers *international* may be a yea word, but for the groups and organizations that receive returnees it is often a nay word that connotes awkward heterogeneity and the absence of an all-important domestic experience. In the Tokugawa period (1600–1868) we find this warning against foreign studies cited from a fief-school code: "Those who take a delight in foreign ways end up by losing their native Japanese spirit and become weakly cowards, a shocking eventuality against which you must ever be on your guard."[12]

The anxiety about the education of children overseas and their return has been perpetuated by the ministry. In several reports and documents the ministry variously defines the issue as learning from the world; training Japanese to take a responsible attitude as citizens of an advanced nation; and readjusting internationalized persons to the domestic system. Some educators see the first definition as a present-day *kaihō* or opening to foreign influence, similar to what occurred in the Meiji period. The second is seen as an assertion of Japanese strengths and recognition of the responsibility Japan ought to bear in an international environment. The third, that international students are a problem for the domestic system, is the one held by the most conservative administrators.[13]

"Learning from the world" is the message carried by a 1976 ministry report.[14] The report urges schools to reduce the pressure on returnee children and thus "eliminate families" worries and let them concentrate on international activities ... to provide a firm basis for Japan's international development." Educational reformers in the mid-1980s echo these sentiments. Although it is hoped that the curriculum will take advantage of the experience of a firsthand "international vision," returnees are seen as a continuing problem, not as the cutting edge in a drive to learn from the world.

The second definition of internationalism is espoused by several private schools. It is expressed, for example, in a study on the education of overseas children authorized by the Ministry of Education and carried out by teachers and administrators associated with Keimei Gakuen, a private school established originally by the Mitsui Company, which receives funds from the ministry for its returnee students.[15] The report encourages parents to enroll their children in local schools abroad and to help them adjust as quickly as possible to the overseas environment. Writers of the report feel that rapid adjustment to foreign ways helps rather than hinders a confident readjustment to Japan. However, there is still a strong feeling that life overseas is difficult for a Japanese: The problems children face overseas lead them to develop strength in adversity, giving them the self-confidence needed to face the difficult readjustment to Japan.[16]

The third definition, which has its followers among several groups associated with the Ministry of Education, reflects the ministry's conservative attitude toward the threats internationalism may pose to domestic education. The Foundation for the Education of Children Overseas (Kaigai Shijo Kyoiku Shinko Zaidan) probably represents the most conservative ministry position. Established by the ministry in 1971, with joint funding from the Foreign Ministry and large corporations, the foundation sets out to "cure the overseas disease." From its offices in Tokyo it arranges predeparture orientation courses, administers overseas Japanese schools and correspondence courses, and provides special counselors for families who have returned from overseas. The counselors also assign returnee children to various readjustment institutions. The latter function determines not just the school a child will attend but his or her entire future. On the basis of an interview and a test a week or two after a child reenters Japan, the counselor may suggest a school from a wide spectrum of possibilities ranging from a normal Japanese school to an intensive "therapeutic" private school.[17]

The foundation also publishes the results of much of the available research on returned children. While academic research is directly supported and published by the Ministry of Education, the more interpretive, advisory publications based on the ministry's data are published by the foundation.[18] The kind of advice given is epitomized in the admonition heading the monthly correspondence course issued by the foundation: "While you are overseas, remember, parents, your children are Japanese," and in the first writing exercise in the text: Hayaku Nihon e kaeritai (I want to return to Japan quickly). Wherever possible, the foundation advises early return (before middle school), maintenance of Japanese language in Japanese schools, the use of correspondence courses, and the fastest possible reintegration of the child into the domestic system after return. If rapid mainstreaming is not possible, the foundation advises admission to so-called "soft" private schools that will take care of those who cannot handle the domestic educational success ladder.

Within the Ministry of Education there is also a faction that supports more open international education. An informally organized group of employees who call themselves the "internationals," they advocate allowing the educational system to create a variety of tracks.[19] Within such a system, the group hopes that returning students would feel less pressure to conform and have a better chance to succeed. The members of the faction—who have had direct overseas experience on loan from the Ministry of Education to UNESCO or other international organizations—have only begun to consider themselves a lobbying force in the past few years and have not had much impact: What change there has been has come come from pressures and influences outside the ministry. Whereas they complain that they are not taken seriously, one ministry official was led to say that even these "radicals" within the ministry are "too Japanese" and identify with the structure of their organization too much to oppose it effectively.

According to the "internationals" and other critics of the ministry, the educational system provides a single-model path to mainstream, generalist careers, as embodied in the life of a white-collar worker in a large company—a "Mitsubishi man" or a member of the "Itoh team." The "internationals" worry especially about the absence of options and the lack of tolerance for any personal differences within the educational system and within individual schools.

In microcosm the range of opinions in the ministry represents the wider ambivalence about diversity or its lack in Japan. Like other contradictions in Japan, this ambivalence comes to rest in a highly fractionated assemblage of perspectives. The diversity of opinion within the Ministry of Education itself reflects the much broader debate on internationalism in Japan, and specifically demonstrates the complexity and confusion about the position of the returnee child.

Schools and Classes for International Children

"Readjustment education," which includes both overseas schools and returnee facilities in Japan, is a relatively recent phenomenon in Japanese education. Other nations—especially Great Britain, France, and the United States—have served the children of their overseas diplomats, colonizers and empire-builders with schools for at least two centuries. Even though Japan began large-scale foreign expansion, military and commercial, as long ago as the 1930s, overseas Japanese communities of business and government workers have only recently become widespread. Since their children must return to the "unique" Japanese educational system and the tightly knit society for which that system trains them, it is clear that without some form of Japanese education overseas or special provisions for reentry, they will suffer severe displacement.

The incentive for the creation of overseas and returnee schools originally came from government ministries and companies whose employees were posted abroad. The Foundation for Overseas Children's Education, funded by both public and private moneys, directs the establishment and curricula of the schools. Most overseas education is funded from outside the Ministry of Education, but special projects, research, and teachers' pay come from a ministry fund for "special education"—a section of the budget also used for facilities for handicapped children.[20]

Overseas Schools

The stated purpose of overseas Japanese education is "to provide education equal to that of the compulsory education system in Japan."[21] Overseas Japanese schools were first established in Manchuria in the late-nineteenth century by companies whose employees were working there. By 1905 the Japanese government had begun to support and coordinate these schools, which then numbered about fifty. Postwar overseas education began in Bangkok in 1956, with a school run by wives of diplomats attached to the Japanese Embassy. In 1983 seventy four full-time Japanese schools served 8,739 children in thirty seven developing and six advanced countries, and there were ninety five supplementary (afternoon and weekend) schools with 8,000 pupils in twenty advanced and eight developing countries. In 1984, 51,000 children between the ages of three and nineteen lived overseas, 28,773 of them in overseas Japanese classes for first through ninth grades, and 7,450 in overseas Japanese high schools (see Figures 1 through 3). Except for one high school in New York City, there is no official overseas education for children younger than six or older than fourteen.

The schools have always been government supported to varying degrees, supplied with teachers and materials sent by the Ministry of Education, but the ministry has recently become concerned about the wide variation in their quality and style of operation. In its April 1976 *Report on Overseas Education* the ministry called for more centralized coordination and control of overseas education to ensure a uniform "domestic Japanese education" for all Japanese children.[22]

September 1975 saw the opening in New York of the first full-time school for Japanese residents. The establishment of this school represented a successful fund-raising venture among businesses and ministries that have employees living in New York. Its founding was also the realization of a new goal: to provide full-time as opposed to supplementary Japanese education even in advanced nations. Hitherto, local schools in advanced nations had been seen as adequate if supplemented by Japanese language lessons, and for that reason such full-time schools had not been seen as necessary in the United States. To support the extension of overseas education, officials at the ministry said that the original purpose of the program had been to provide a high-quality curriculum but that it had now changed to provide Japanese-style education overseas—something no local school could provide, no matter how advanced its society and culture. The Ministry of Education states that it is responsible for providing all Japanese children with a Japanese education—implicitly, one that will ensure their acceptability and survival in Japanese society and organizations.

The lack of uniform centralized organization and the low priority and status given to overseas teaching assignments have caused problems for these schools. Parents have many complaints about the quality of education that their children receive, most based on the criticism that the schools don't sufficiently resemble mainstream Japanese

Figure 1
Japanese Children's Use of Overseas Educational Facilities, by Region

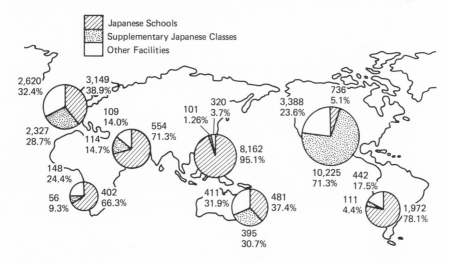

Source: Ministry of Education, *Overseas Children's Education* (Tokyo: Ministry of Education, February 1985).

Figure 2
Numbers and Percentages of Japanese Children Overseas by Area, February 1985

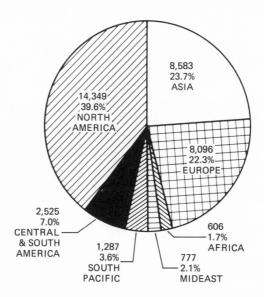

Source: Ministry of Education, *Overseas Children's Education* (Tokyo: Ministry of Education, February 1985).

Figure 3
Use of Overseas Education Facilities by Japanese Children, 1975–84

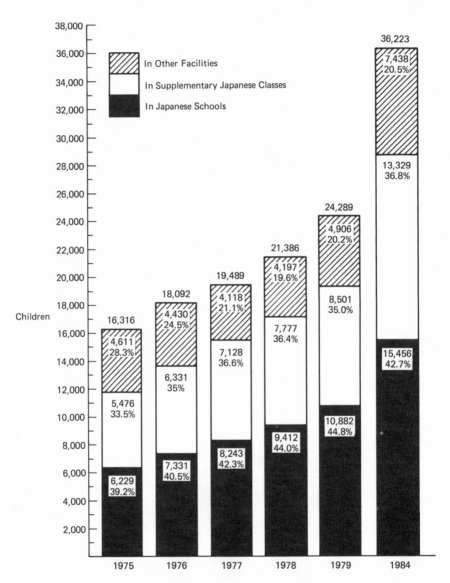

Source: Ministry of Education, *Overseas Children's Education* (Tokyo: Ministry of Education, February 1985).

schools. Many say that because teachers in these schools are from remote areas of Japan, their children cannot learn a standard Tokyo accent, and they repeatedly aver that the schools are not well run, that morale is low, and that discipline is nonexistent. They point to the fact that administrators are not selected from the pool of candidates trained to run schools in Japan but are often drawn from among recently retired ministry bureaucrats—people who have often had little experience either as teachers or as school administrators.[22]

In places where the overseas Japanese community has been especially active and forceful in shaping an educational program, parental fears have produced schools that are assertively separatist and ethnocentric. A more truly international-minded Japanese overseas community would not pour its energies into an overseas school. In fact, at the moment, an "international overseas Japanese school" is a contradiction in terms. Japanese overseas education attempts to protect children against a loss of "Japanese" skills or behavior patterns and, most important, against the acquisition of behaviors and skills inappropriate to Japanese life. As the drive toward success in Japan becomes more intense, the differentness implied by a non-Japanese education becomes more threatening, leading some overseas families to demand better Japanese facilities for their children. It is still hard to be both a Japanese parent and an "international person."

Readjustment Education

The education received by returnee children takes several forms. Although their numbers are still relatively small, much attention is given to them, and several options for their reintroduction to Japan exist. About eight thousand Japanese children return home every year, and about four out of every ten thousand pupils in elementary and secondary schools are recent returnees (those who have been back less than two years). In spite of their relatively low numbers, the school system has made them highly visible. First, the concentration of returnees in Tokyo and surrounding regions (in 1979, 69 percent of the total) makes them more of a factor than their numbers alone would indicate. The fact that the population of returnees is geographically concentrated in or near the capital means that government and business policymakers responsible for the problms are more aware of them. A second and related factor is that the parents themselves, especially those employed by large companies and prestigious ministries, are often influential people who can reach those who are able to give the problem high-level consideration. The companies and the ministries employing these high-profile returnees have participated most actively in the establishment of readjustment classes.

Facilities for returnee education are usually jointly funded by public and private organizations. Ministry-established public returnee classes are usually held in classrooms in regular schools but may be in separate buildings. As of February 1985, such public facilities included forty three elementary schools, thirty nine middle schools, and forty four high schools (some with partial private funding). Several are in schools attached to national universities and serve as laboratories for educational research. Meanwhile, some wards and cities have established their own programs (see Appendix 2). Whether private or public, however, all readjustment schools concentrate on those aspects of the curriculum seen as most characteristically Japanese: language, math, and social studies. All provide remedial language work and intensive academic counseling on appropriate educational and occupational goals.

Among the full-time readjustment schools subsidized by the Ministry of Education is the Hatano Family School in Mejiro, Tokyo, founded in 1973. In 1984 approximately fifty children were enrolled in its full-time program, with about two hundred more in weekend readjustment classes. The school provides an intensive adjustment program and admits the most extreme reentry cases, including children who were born and educated wholly outside Japan. There are also a few children of mixed marriages. The average period of attendance at this school is about one year, but it claims that in "less serious" cases, a child of elementary school age can enter a regular public school after three months of intensive work.

Through its foundation and counselors, the ministry actively encourages parents to use private "receiving" or cooperating schools.[24] This puts the burden of caring for these students on private schools that may receive compensation from the ministry as "support for readjustment programs."[25] Some private school administrators have said that such funding relieves the ministry of the need to establish a more integrated and uniform public readjustment system or to undertake more drastic reform of the regular schools.

The burden of educating returnees has also fallen on some schools that are unable to win accreditation from the Ministry of Education. These schools, called "nonregular special schools" (kakushu gakkoo),[26] do not follow ministry-prescribed curricula. Moreover, the parents of children who attend these schools must pay periodic fines for not sending their children to accredited schools. Recently, one of them, an international school located in Tokyo's "embassy row," has actively fought with the ministry to gain accreditation. Its Japanese students come from a variety of backgrounds ranging from shopkeeper families to relatives of the emperor. The Japanese children represent only 10 percent of the school population, but their parents are very vocal and often influential people. Other such schools, with larger percentages of Japanese children, may have more chance of success with the ministry. To gain recognition from the ministry, these schools can exert pressure because of the numbers of returnees they care for. In other words, the currently unaccredited schools may eventually acquire official sanction by taking care of students whom the system rejects. One long-range consequence may be the introduction of diversity into the Japanese educational system, and yet that diversity may only be tolerated in a compartmentalized form.

Signs of Readjustment

Children are placed in readjustment schools after consultations with public schools teachers or with counselors at the Foundation for Overseas Children's Education. The children are tested at the time of school entrance and at regular intervals thereafter in the three critical subjects. At the same time, they are reintroduced to other aspects of Japanese life: morning radio exercises, classroom behavior and routines, customs such as removal of outdoor footwear and the use of soft indoor shoes, and the maintenance of a respectful mien towards persons who are older or of higher status. The performance of such Japanese behaviors is felt to be as necessary as Japanese language ability or mathematical skill, and there is little tolerance for persistent deviation. A domestic grade-schooler who occasionally forgets to change his shoes or who is rude to a teacher is corrected but forgiven because "boys will be boys" (girls are expected to have better manners). But a returnee who does the same things with the same frequency is watched closely, and his rudeness is attributed to the overseas sojourn. In short, signs of cultural differentness may be indications of a lapse of identity but are not in themselves problems for those who are not "suspect." A Japanese who has never sojourned abroad may grow his hair long, develop a taste for Indian food, or dot his speech with English words without arousing much suspicion, but if a returnee displays such habits, he is seen as cosmopolitan and different. In fact, of course, the Japanese are ready borrowers of Western cultural modes. It is only when a borrowed cultural trait may symbolize a member's physical and temporal absence from the group that it becomes a problem.

Teachers interviewed often said that returnees have no "Japanese common sense." As one said, "We cannot figure out just what it is that is missing in them. It is a kind of Japaneseness. They see it all around them—on TV and in their friends' behavior—but they cannot have it themselves." Teachers also complain that these children aren't *genki* (healthy and energetically active), that they don't know how to exert themselves. Some even worry that girls who have lived overseas have strayed so far from the norm that they will not be marriageable. Returnees are given pejorative epithets such as *hen japa* or *han japa* ("strange Japanese" or "half-Japanese")—phrases that use a form of the *English*, not the Japanese, word for *Japanese*. These epithets are semijokingly used by the returnees against themselves, much as members of American minorities sometimes use derogatory racial epithets among themselves.

Akira Hoshino, a psychologist specializing in the phenomenon of culture shock, quotes a girl who returned from the Middle East to Japan: "When I returned to my motherland, small children chased me and shouted out, 'Oh, here is a gaikokujin [foreigner]!' At [a returnee] school I was overwhelmed with joy when I found 'strange Japanese' similar to me, and teachers who understood us."

Hoshino noted, "It is hard for native Japanese to relate to those Japanese children who, though they physically appear the same, return home with different views and values. These children are neither immigrants nor of an ethnic or political minority, and yet they are thorns in the side of the native group. Teachers may ignore these children, or may single them out as bad examples. In some cases, teachers may even show some antagonism towards these students."[27] Whether or not teachers are predisposed to see these children as unable to adjust, the watchfulness that surrounds returnees' every action clearly makes their adjustment an uphill battle.

The problem is exacerbated for high-school-age returnees, for whom there are few publicly funded facilities. Compared to younger students, fewer in this age group travel overseas, and those who do tend to opt for international colleges in Japan or universities abroad. For children who return to middle or high school in Japan there are about ninety private schools that have special facilities, such as counselors and remedial language classes or that are willing to admit returnees though they have no special facilities. The fifty with special programs are clustered around the Tokyo and Osaka areas. These private schools, called "receiving" or "cooperating" schools, are informally known as "soft" schools. International Christian University in Tokyo recently established a high school especially to accommodate returnees and to help them prepare for Japanese universities. One teacher there referred ironically to the tasks and expectations involved, saying, "They come there to think, not to memorize, but in a year they are tamed." An investigation of the student population of such schools for returnees shows that their students are predominately of high school age, although middle school students are attending in increasing numbers.[28]

According to counselors and teachers, the older the returnee, the more trouble he or she will have in the examinations and the more trouble in adjusting to the Japanese school system. Older children are thus more apt to be placed in special schools than are younger children. A comparison of the total number of middle-school-age returnees with middle school attendance at receiving schools shows a striking discrepancy. Whereas 71 percent of returning children are of middle school age, only 32 percent of the receiving schools' population is of middle school age. The percentages of high-school-age children are the reverse: Twenty-nine percent of the returnees are of high school age, but 68 percent of the receiving school population is of high school age. This seems to indicate that younger children are not seen as requiring special treatment as much as those confronted with the examinations. It appears also that parents of high-school-age children returning to Japan may prefer not to pit them against classmates who have no "handicap" and choose instead the isolation of "readjustment," or "soft," education.

The children in this study's sample attended four types of schools after returning to Japan: ordinary public schools, ordinary private schools, government-sponsored readjustment schools, and private international schools (see appendix 3 for sample characteristics).

Thirty-seven percent of all respondents used readjustment classes. A breakdown by sex shows that while 49 percent of the girls used overseas Japanese classes or correspondence courses, as opposed to only 31 percent of the boys, nearly the opposite situation exists for readjustment schools in Japan, with 57 percent of the boys using them as opposed to 19 percent of the girls. Although the figures relating to the use of Japanese lessons overseas seem to belie the professed relaxed attitude of parents toward the internationalization of their daughters, figures relating to the use of re-entry programs show that anxiety over the return to Japan forces parents to enroll sons more than daughters in public and private readjustment facilities. Boys are expected to conform more rigorously than girls, who are permitted a more relaxed "international flavor." In fact, parents considering a profession or work for their daughters often say that they will have greater opportunities for interesting work as translators and in other international areas that they would not see as worthy for their sons.

The Child Overseas and at Home: Preparation for the Overseas Sojourn

As the case of the Ishidas shows, even before the family's departure from Japan, anxiety and pressure mount that will affect the child and his or her family at home and abroad. Relatives, friends, and teachers warn children that their lives will be very different overseas and alert families to the danger of culture shock. In publications distributed by the Foundation for Overseas Children's Education to parents about to be transferred overseas, there are specific instructions about how to prepare children for the overseas stay. First, parents are advised on how to separate their children gradually from their Japanese friends so that they won't "pine away" as a result of the sudden reality of removal. In most cases the father is sent ahead to get housing and to make school arrangements. He is advised to write to his wife and children about local customs. Publications warn him to be alert to such things as whether children bring lunch to school, change shoes at school, pledge allegiance to a flag, and so on. This preliminary scouting is necessary, for, "since customs are different, the Japanese child may be laughed at." Parents are also advised that foreign children may not be able to pronounce their children's names, and so they may want to adopt foreign nicknames for their stay abroad, such as Ken or Mike. They should help their child learn proper forms of address and customs of greeting. Although the tone of the publications is gentle and concerned, mothers felt that they were more worried *after* they read these warnings than before, and some said that they wished that the Japanese wouldn't make so much fuss about overseas sojourns.

More dramatic warnings are contained in some of the lectures in a predeparture family orientation program sponsored by the foundation.

The lecture on overseas education given by a circuit lecturer demonstrated the mood and content of several talks in the series. The message was that overseas educational life is fraught with dangers that even the most conscientious parent cannot ameliorate.[29] The lecturer dramatized his points with blackboard sketches of a cartoon-style Japanese child holding a pen in his hand. He concluded his remarks by saying, "When you travel overseas, your child will not be able to see Japanese characters, and he will become unused to seeing his own language"—as he crossed out the cartoon child's eyes—"and when your child cannot hear Japanese spoken, he will become deaf to his language"—as he crossed out the ears. He moved on in similar fashion to the mouth and the pen-holding hand and finished in dramatic tones, saying, "With so many problems, a Japanese child overseas, after as little as three months, can suffer a nervous breakdown"—at which he crossed out the child's heart. There were audible gasps from the audience. He then proposed the use of overseas schools, correspondence courses (which are provided by the foundation), and, for children who were old enough, leaving them with relatives in Japan. The mothers learned the lesson of fear well; one said, by way of a nervous joke, that she would rather get a divorce than take her children overseas.

Another lecturer later in the series tried in vain to persuade her audience that life overseas is exciting and enriching for the child. She was depressed by the mothers' subsequent demands for "remedies" for the effects of an overseas sojourn. In general, however, the lecturers gave their audiences what they expected to hear—the message that they and their children would experience various problems as Japanese overseas and that these problems could be minimized by careful maintenance of a Japanese education and life-style. The ideal is analogous to the strategy used by some people who frequently travel across time zones and keep their watches and lives on "home time" as much as possible, avoiding jet lag by trying to avoid sleeping according to the "real time" of their new locale.

Some publications concentrate on the physical hardships of overseas life and engender the sense that the outside world is a dangerous and uncaring place. One such article, by a panel of Japanese doctors, was published in Japan Airlines' *Family Service Bulletin*. The doctors discussed the health problems Japanese might face because of climate or dietary conditions overseas. They also suggested that Japanese children might develop ailments as a result of social or cultural problems encountered living overseas. Finally, the doctors assert, "In foreign cities Japanese tend to have few friends, and various mental and emotional problems are increased. This leads to a poor appetite and unbalanced diet, and in children it is called 'children's nervous disease.' "

Overseas Life

In spite of their worries, only a very small number of parents reported that their children had persistent difficulties adjusting to overseas life, no matter where they were located. It is, in fact, easy to leave.

Based on reports by informants, it is possible to discern four stages of a child's adjustment overseas: (1) immersion, or an immediate and uncritical absorption and interest in the local environment; (2) comparison, choice, and commitment, either to Japan or "overseas"; and, just before returning to Japan, (3) rejection of the most un-Japanese characteristics of overseas life; and (4) retrenchment, or conscious protection of Japanese culture. One informant, who was twelve at the time of her move to the United States, described her life in California in these terms:

> My first reaction was to fall in love with everything—open friends, going barefoot to the ice-cream parlor. I became fluent in English. . . . Then I became severely critical of Japan and approved all American ways. I labeled Japan as narrow-minded. . . . Then [two years later] I became aware that I was, after all, a foreigner [and] felt alone, and intentionally cut myself off from school activities. . . . I began to feel glad to have an intimate Japanese family life, the feeling that my parents, my sister, and I were one body the way I did not feel in the homes of my American friends. I was a teenager and I needed to know who I was. . . . I began to have Japanese foreign students as my friends and had a new emotional attachment to Japan.

Except for three children in the sample, all were fluent in the local language after three to six months overseas. The three—the only ones reported to have had any major overseas adjustment problems—were small boys who refused to speak a foreign langauge. Only one girl was reported to have had school problems overseas, and she was later diagnosed in Japan as dyslexic.

Children generally remember about their overseas experience that there was more time for family outings and after-school play. Classes in most cases were smaller than classes in Japan and homework was light. Except for supplementary Japanese language classes, which were used by 40 percent of the children, there were no tutors or after-school lessons, and many children began hobbies or new sports activities.[30]

The International Child in School, Peer Group, and Family

Fitting into a society in which an outside experience is at best irrelevant and at worst stigmatizing is most difficult for returning children. Children are under strong pressure from the community to be "normal." The experiences of the children returning to Japanese schools reflect the confusion and anxiety surrounding the introduction of diversity into a conservative and homogeneous system. The unpredictability implied in such children's assumed differentness is particularly threatening in a Japanese classroom. First, classes are large, with only one teacher on average for forty-two children. The teacher must stop the class and persuade a student who does not behave appropriately to cooperate. The spirit of harmony the teacher can expect from children who have been socialized to a Japanese classroom may not be present in a returnee. So he or she may need to use more extreme or overt methods, which may single out the offending outsider unable to pick up the teacher's cues. Meanwhile, returnees who don't join or attempt to join the group are labeled "selfish." If they talk too much in class, they are seen as assertive. If they greet their friends or teachers in a casual, American-style manner, they will be shunned. Since social behavior is an implicit part of the curriculum, such manifestations are the teacher's responsibility to correct.

Further, taking time to work with "special cases" slows down the group's progress, making it harder to maintain standards of achievement as well as group cohesion. Because special attention from the teacher would be a problem even with a nonreturnee population, among whom it would be seen as favoritism, some teachers have "paired" returnees with "normal" students, who act as peer counselors. As pairing has become a common practice, however, the other students may begin to feel the returnee as a burden. Worse, the returnee may hurt the class as a whole, by lowering its average level of performance, at least when the returnee is catching up to grade level. One returnee girl reported:

> My class used to be the top among ten classes of the same age. When the teacher told us that we had become second . . . I felt as though my classmates were accusing me of bringing them down. Indeed, the class leader came to me and said, very gently, that I should study harder since everybody else's efforts in this class would become

worthless.... I became guilty and ashamed that I was a burden to the class."[31]

The readjustment classes and schools were established to relieve the ordinary classroom of the initial problems of return, but as we have seen, they give the returnee a mixed message. On the one hand, they encourage rapid reassimilation of Japanese skills and habits, while on the other, they seem to convey to returnee children that they are already impossibly different, that conformity is not possible.

That message is reinforced by a child's peer group. Like children everywhere, Japanese children are keen observers of detail and notice anything out of the ordinary. If one of their number wears something unusual, brings a different sort of lunch to school, or talks or behaves in a strange way, he or she will be teased by the others and exposed to great pressure to conform. This teasing sometimes assumes violent and physical form in *ijime*, or bullying, and makes the "odd one" feel permanently stigmatized: It is hard for returnees to feel confident that they will ever be accepted by the group. Children in the sample reported that their classmates called them "foreigner" and that they were closely watched for signs of deviance. Children who at first insisted on retaining some signs of their overseas stay—such as eating peanut butter sandwiches for lunch or wearing foreign lace-up sneakers instead of elasticized Japanese ones—quickly adopted Japanese habits in response to teasing from other children or pressure from their parents. One boy wore an American printed sweatshirt to school until he was teased out of it by classmates who kept calling him an Eskimo, even though similar sweatshirts were being sold all over Tokyo at the time. Returnee mothers interviewed claimed that teasing of this sort is encouraged by the mothers of nonreturnee children, who point out such subtle differences to their offspring. Teachers often send notes home encouraging mothers to help their children readjust faster by adhering more closely to Japanese customs. One mother, whose child refused to eat the usual Japanese lunch and insisted on making his own sandwiches, received a note asking her to help her child by providing a "Japanese mother's healthful lunch."

Some young children were puzzled when adults objected to their "overseas style." When asked at his school's opening ceremonies to make the traditional formal greeting to teachers and classmates, a first-grade returnee responded by swaggering up to the microphone in the manner of a U.S. television master of ceremonies. In Japanese sprinkled with English he told a shaggy-dog story of his experiences with bears in Yellowstone Park, until a teacher took the microphone away.

He had not known what was expected of him and was surprised at the teasing he later suffered.

Some children who had been overseas a long time or had lived in developing countries tried to reassimilate rapidly. They did not talk about their overseas experience with their friends because, as they said, "I don't want to seem strange," and worked hard to learn Japanese playground games and songs. One girl had hoped her Japanese friends would want to hear of her European experiences but quickly stopped talking about them, since the others said she was "showing off":

> The group leader finally said I could join the group if I promised not to talk about Europe. ... After this experience, I decided never to talk about it, and whenever I talked I asked myself whether I was being conspicuous or not. Gradually I began to hate my European experience. If only I had not gone there! ... I would not have experienced this pain. ... By rejecting my overseas experience, I started to assimilate to Japan.[32]

Two children were reported to have developed very aggressive "nationalistic" hobbies after returning: One devoted himself to learning all the battles of World War II and the other to building models of Japanese warships. These were children of academics who did not themselves attempt such reassimilation, somewhat to the embarrassment of the children, who—it might be said—were trying to compensate for their parents' unconventionality.

Another strategy by which children, like adults, make themselves more comfortable in Japan is to find friends among others who have been away or among children who for other reasons seem different. Most say they feel happier with other returnees, and all children in the readjustment schools say they are happier there than playing in their neighborhoods. A returnee girl who attends a regular school in Tokyo has developed a close friendship with a girl who was raised in Osaka, whom others teased for her "strange foreign accent"—a dialect common to the Osaka region. The returnee said that she felt very protective of the Osaka girl because others had teased her in the same way. The both of them were called gaijin by their classmates.

A particularly ironic adjustment is often made by returnee students who have learned English overseas and return to Japanese English classes. Because of peer pressure, they must "forget" their "foreign" English and adapt to Japanese-style English. One girl who learned English in the Netherlands from a British teacher felt painfully out of place speaking excellent English in Japan—her classmates teased her.

Her teacher in Japan sadly noted, "What happened to you? Your pronunciation was very good when you came back from Holland. But now it's the same as that of the other students."[33] In spite of the teacher's regret, the student saw this as praise for her readjustment to "Japanese English."

The Foundation for Overseas Children's Education also runs "English maintenance classes" for returnees who want to keep up their English learned overseas. Several informants attended the classes and complained that the style of instruction and texts used had little relation to their children's level of ability and experiences. The real purpose, they said, was to convert English learned overseas to what they admitted was more useful in Japan, "examination English," which stresses vocabulary, rules of grammar, and sentence structure. The training fits in well with the standard multiple-choice examination, since it teaches isolable pieces of information about English, rather than general conversational fluency, which is harder to test. As a guest, I taught a sixth-grade English maintenance class in a readjustment school and found the children bored and restless with the materials, which were multiple-choice tests with all directions and explanations given in Japanese. The children spent time talking about returnee problems and complained that they did very poorly in English, which wasn't fair, since all the directions were in Japanese.

Lack of Japanese language proficiency is regarded as one of the most significant markers of disability. Teachers say that in Japan, language is tightly bound to social and cultural identity. One teacher said "two languages mean two cultures—it is hard for a Japanese child."

Several language-usage markers determine how well integrated a returnee is. One is polite language, in which a person changes forms of speech according to his or her position vis-à-vis the interlocutor. Another is male and female language, by which even small children assert themselves or distinguish themselves from the opposite sex. One of the more subtle forms of readjustment involves how well a child picks up playground language—chants, talk, slang—and a specialized kind of Japanese expressive language used by all ages—the giseigo, or onomatopoetic language. Words such as pochapocha, (chubby), gobogobo (gurgle of water), and zuruzuru (slippery) are not slang or baby talk, but an integral part of the language and must be relearned before one is considered fully reintegrated. Teachers in the readjustment schools have special songs and games to help children learn such words.

Another problem is the standardization of physical education.

Although children might have had sports overseas, they would not have learned the routinized exercise drills of Japanese schools. Parents reported that boys especially felt embarrassed over this, leading some to feel quite inferior to others.

Although not all families use the readjustment schools and classes, all are aware of the perils involved in ignoring the problems of reentry. Attendance at an overseas Japanese school is not considered a guarantee that a child may pass into a regular school. On the contrary, parents who have placed their children in such schools are often the most eager to use readjustment classes as well. In fact, use of both seems to correlate more strongly with parental anxiety than it does with the actual efficacy of the schools to produce the "normal" Japanese children that most returnee mothers and fathers want their children to be.

Parents of children who are teased, excluded, or pointed to as different often see the problem as a sign of their own inability to raise their children as Japanese. The more encouragement the teachers give, the more special attention the children receive, the more anxious some parents become. According to counselors, children of such parents suffer the most from psychosomatic disorders after returning to Japan. In my sample, three families reported that their children had "evening rashes"; two families said that their children had insomnia; and many children were reported to be depressed and exhausted.

Indeed, both parents and the media have used a vocabulary of victimization and disease to describe the children's condition. Parents and counselors interviewed in a newspaper article[34] said that the children suffer from "serious illnesses" and have "dreadful wounds" (*kizutsuita ko*) and that the readjustment schools are "treatment centers for difficult cases. . . . The schools seem like hospitals for curing children who have fallen ill with 'foreign-language-itis' and aim to make them into 'Japanese.'" For one mother, having her daughter treated as "ill" seemed better than having her branded as different. She preferred the international section in a private school where her daughter "is treated just like a handicapped child; the teachers and pupils both recognized her need for special care"[35] and refrained from the teasing and harsh discipline she might have gotten in an ordinary school.

Parents respond to readjustment education in a variety of ways, depending on their goals. Those who hope that their children will be "100 percent Japanese" may be pleased with the attention that their children receive in an international section but worry that it is only catching-up education and that their children will never be so competitive in the examination race. Other parents, who had hoped that their children might preserve the language skills and broader vision acquired overseas, were also disappointed in the readjustment classes. As a parent said of one school, "It is not an international school. It is really intended to wash the international color out of the children and re-Japanize them."

Some parents choose to immerse their children directly in regular schools, with as few fellow returnees in their classes as possible. But these parents must be careful in the choice of ordinary schools. Those who hope their children can enter top universities will try to move to a good urban school district with a prestigious school. Others feel their children will do better in more relaxed schools and choose a suburban or exurban environment. Parents who live in smaller cities, with smaller returnee populations, report that their children have less trouble than those in Tokyo.[36]

Urban or suburban parents may choose schools that have no special facilities and small populations of returnees, hoping their children will be absorbed more quickly into ordinary school life. However, where there are more than three returnees, teachers report that they tend to cluster and form a clique and that readjustment problems are greater. Parents are torn between sending their children to schools where they might readjust quickly without special help or to schools where they might be placed in a returnee "ghetto" but where there would be teachers and facilities to help them.

Readjustment and the Future of the Child

Parents in general trust the Japanese educational system to provide a well-orchestrated present and a secure future for their children and suffer a shock when they are cast adrift overseas. Japanese schools and weekend classes help make them feel that they are doing what they can to bridge the gap. But as their children gradually speak less and less Japanese even at home, and as letters come from friends telling of the long study hours their children put in at home and in juku, parents abroad become anxious about their children's chances in Japan.

Arriving home, they accept the verdict that extra work is needed before their children can be admitted as normal Japanese students. If a child is too old and has missed too many years of "examination education," the parents have to come to terms with the child's handicap, often with as much sense of tragedy as if it were physical. The child is regarded as having been derailed from the Japanese track; sent to international or special private schools, he or she faces an eccentric or uncertain future in Japan. Courses presently open to these children include careers as translators and interpreters, liaison staff, media workers, and technicians involved in foreign aid—all involving direct use of the specialization that has branded them. Special dispensations, such as English-language entrance exams to returnee high schools, special quotas for returnees in certain universities, or guaranteed employment in the international bureau of a father's company do not reduce the burden of stigma.

Few Japanese of any occupation would feel easy about taking chances with their children's future. Accordingly, mainstream people, who all their lives supported the consensus that education is the only key to success, feel their children's displacement most keenly. Up to the point of their overseas sojourn they have represented the model life path: a good education, a secure job in a large corporation, and a carefully planned family present and future. There is some irony in the fact that the mainstream organizations that give parents their status are, by sending them overseas, endangering the children's position in the educational system and perhaps denying them a mainstream future in Japan.

I have described education in Japan as a strongly conservative system that stresses the importance of single-path conformity and hard work and reinforces a special Japanese style of group membership. The tolerance within such a system for differentness of any kind is clearly very low, and the sensitivity to aberrations, however slight, is very high. The system, in other words, has little internal flexibility: There is a single curriculum, a single pace, and by and large a single goal—passing university examinations. For those children with a different background who need time to catch on or up, or who may have adopted different patterns of behavior, or who have unconventional goals, the Japanese school is a most uncomfortable place. Teachers and classmates may hover over the child whose Japanese language is not "pure" or whose arithmetic was learned from a different textbook. Although the emphasis on conformity and the avoidance of distinctions in the classroom prevent schools from holding children back or placing them with a younger age group, the returnee puts a serious strain on the practice. A teacher may try to accelerate readjustment by telling the child and his or her parents in so many words to forget the overseas experience. In any case, the child is made aware of being different, and the family is made to feel that its overseas stay was a dangerous hiatus in its children's lives.

The Ministry of Education, as I have already indicated, follows several courses of action, all based on the schools' need for uniformity and on their anxiety about differentness. Some of its programs isolate and mark returnees as international, and others attempt to erase signs of the overseas experience. In all the schools, counseling services, and classes, the underlying feeling is the same: Returnee children represent both a threat and a pitiable case. They are a threat because the schools and teachers feel they cannot train children successfully in a diverse or pluralistic atmosphere. They are pitiable because those who possess a "mixed" background are thought for that reason to be unhappy and uncomfortable and in need of help to overcome the situation before they are permanently marked as outsiders.

5

Adult Strategies: Mothers and Fathers at Home and at Work

Parents are not as obviously watched, protected and stigmatized as are their children on return to Japan. Why? Because of the simple fact that, at least in a structural sense, they already belong. While children are at high risk on the meritocratic and highly structured ladder of success, their parents have found their places. But the places still demand much of those who occupy them, and the culture of work and relationships in Japan puts great pressure on adult returnees. Although there are no "readjustment classes" for parents, fathers at work and mothers in the community must reschool themselves in Japanese common sense, just as their children are trained in school. Toward this end, various strategies and options are available to returnee parents.

Mothers Abroad

We have looked briefly at the lives of three women overseas. Mrs. Hayashi, Mrs. Kajima, and Mrs. Fujimura share a total commitment to their children; in Japan, both the daily life of the household and the structure of the family regard the mother-child relationship as central. But what about the women themselves? Even the ideal woman, at home in Japan, does things other than child rearing, and for some, the overseas experience widens their interests beyond the family. Usually, however, the woman's immediate return to Japan is colored most strongly by family worries, no matter how much, as in Mrs. Hayashi's case, she may want to pursue her own interests and career. Several women in the sample took courses in local colleges or adult education centers, which led them to consider returning to school for an advanced degree. Few took jobs; usually visa restrictions precluded this. But the women who did work often used their Japanese skills: They taught language courses and held flower-arranging or cooking classes.

The greatest difference lay in their relationships with their husbands, for most reported that their husbands were home much more than they had been in Japan. At the beginning of an overseas stay, this may be very welcome; the mother, often isolated, has more difficulty than her husband and children in adjusting to foreign life, especially since she has little to structure her days and provide her with a community. Compared to her life in Japan, she may be rather helpless: she has difficulty with language, she may find herself in a home no longer within walking distance of shops (in American suburbs, for example, she must often rely on her husband to do the marketing for her), she has difficulty understanding her children's educational experience, and—if she has few acquaintances—she may be very lonely.

One setting that poses particular difficulty for Japanese women is the doctor's office or medical clinic. Japanese women living abroad have been known to delay treatment because of anxieties about communicating with foreign doctors. In Japan it is not customary for patients to become involved in their own treatment or to discuss or question a doctor's diagnosis. The suggestions of a foreign doctor are therefore likely to be taken as directives. Occasionally, however, Japanese patients will accept a prescription but not take non-Japanese medication because they feel that it is not appropriate to the "unique" Japanese physiology.[1]

Once adjusted to life overseas, however, the Japanese woman may be better able than her husband to take advantage of her new environment. She may emerge as the better linguist, especially if her husband works in a wholly Japanese office. She may develop new hobbies and have more everyday contact with people in the local community, especially in the United States or Europe. However, the situation in developing countries, where the Japanese communities are more insular, may be quite different. Here she will have to get used to a "colonial" life style.[2] She may have a household of servants to direct, who may be the only local people she knows well. She may almost never use language other than Japanese, unless it is English in the company of international business or diplomatic families. As in Japan, her husband will not participate in housework or family decisions, but she must rely almost exclusively on him for companionship. Their children probably attend a Japanese school and lead a purely Japanese life. But there are differences between life in a Japanese enclave overseas and life in Japan, as one mother related:

> In the Philippines, we had many servants. I had a lot of free time, but there was no work I could do and it would have seemed strange to work. I played golf every day or went to tea parties with other Japanese women. We all drove around in large cars with chauffeurs, and life was very easy. But the women were very snobby and exclusive and even had their own language—a kind of superpolite, prewar women's talk, in which they exaggerated everything. At first I thought it was silly and even a little disgusting, but I gradually began to use it.

Though some women who had lived in several overseas locales commented that they were more immersed in the society and culture of advanced nations than of developing ones, they also found differences among the former. Those who had been to both Europe and the United States said that it was easier for them to remain Japanese in Europe than in the United States. They perceive European society as traditional and status oriented, which, they say, was both comfortable for them as they came from a similar society, and prevented them from getting deeply involved in the local community. However, they felt that their differentness was respected even if kept at arm's length. Americans, on the other hand, seemed to expect them to adopt American customs, and sometimes they were "forced" out of the home into social activities by well-meaning acquaintances. A sojourn in continental Europe does present a language problem, however. The fact that all Japanese learn some English in school means that Japanese overseas may be more comfortable in countries where English is spoken. Women often began foreign language classes overseas, but only a few became fluent in languages other than English.

Some internal constraints were reported within the Japanese community overseas. Women felt that their Japanese contacts were excessively limited by their husband's occupations. Bankers' wives, for instance, were doubly isolated—first from the local population and second from nonbanking families in the Japanese overseas community. The banking husbands did not play golf with manufacturing or trading company men, nor did their wives see much of nonbanker wives. Academic families, on the other hand, reported that they tried to avoid a "Japanese ghetto life" and often made energetic attempts to meet local families by organizing tea parties, children's parties, and neighborhood lessons in flower arrangement.

The experience common to all the women of the sample, regardless of where they lived overseas or their husbands' occupations, was that of being mothers of school-age children. Although they were much less involved with local schools and met with teachers much less frequently than in Japan, they remained as close or became closer to their children than they had been in Japan. The time they spent coaching them depended on how much anxiety they felt over the return to Japan, which in turn depended on how old the children were and thus how close to the crucial entrance examinations. With materials brought from Japan, or with correspondence courses sent monthly from Japan, they worked an average of six hours per week with each child. (Some spent as much as two hours per day.) Some also attempted to help with the work of the local schools, but they were often hindered by language barriers. However, most mothers helped children only with their Japanese homework, and they often could not say what the children studied in the overseas local schools.

Return to Japan

After returning to Japan, a mother's first task is to help her children readjust to Japanese education. As Kumiko Hayashi threw herself into the "returned education mama" role, so the mother is the bridge to the educational system and the target audience for the predeparture educational orientation programs. She is called the "home tutor" or the "teacher's ally" and in general is seen as the person in the family responsible for linking the returning child to the school. Thus, immediately after returning she is busy with visits to counselors, schools, juku, and testing centers. Some mothers even reported that they put off calling on close relatives or friends after returning to Japan, giving as the very acceptable excuse the primary need to arrange for their children's educational rerentry. This may take days or weeks of paperwork, travel, and waiting-room and interview time.

When the mother's task of placing her children in schools is accomplished, she then faces her own readjustment, which is often rather complex. Some women enjoy the "freedom" to arrange and control family matters and the time they have to themselves in Japan. Unlike families overseas, Japanese rarely entertain at home. This is a relief to many returnee women, and they are rather glad that their husbands are away many hours each day. But those who adopted an American family style feel that in Japan they have the worst of both worlds.

Their family life must now follow a Japanese pattern of role separation, but they do not like the sharp separation of tasks and spheres of
control. One woman who had lived in Australia said that she now
hated being a "wife-style person" in Japan. She wished she could pursue a theatrical career, but said that the neighbors would talk about
her if she were to attend rehearsals even when the children were in
school. She also lamented the fact that "there are no baby-sitters in
Japan."

Among other problems women experienced was that of readjustment to the finely modulated dress code in Japan. Women who had
lived overseas for long periods of time, especially in Europe or North
America, tended to dress according to local fashions, though they usually chose clothing they hoped would be acceptable in Japan too. In
Japan, after children are born, women change to a distinctly more conservative style in clothing, hair, and cosmetics.[3] By contrast, in the
United States and Europe there is more continuity between the stages
of a woman's life in terms of dress. Japanese women who buy clothing
overseas often dress in styles that are considered "too youthful" or
"informal" for their age and role. When women in the sample wear
hade (loud) colors or styles, they are seen as strange and too obviously
different in Japan. (As I mentioned, Mrs. Kajima put away her elegant
European fur coat when she returned to Japan.)

On their return to Japan, some women complain of isolation from
other women in their communities, which they feel is partly imposed
on them. One woman, a free-lance journalist working at home, says
she has no one to talk with and is trying to find another returnee family
in the neighborhood. She has "given up" on women in her community, saying: "One day, I decided that I wasn't going to try any longer.
They are polite to me, but they treat me like a foreigner. So I decided
to *be* a foreigner to them, and I decided to wear my bright red slacks
which I bought in the U.S. Now they really don't talk to me."

Since she has already been excluded, hers may be nothing more
than a sour grapes gesture, but she has chosen a somewhat unusual
exhibitionism. Such women choose to be with foreigners as much as
possible, yet they rarely introduce their foreign friends to their Japanese friends.

Relationships with relatives often change after the return to Japan,
especially of wives with their mothers-in-law. Women complained
most often that their obligations to their mothers-in-law had become
terrible burdens. A traditional woman is expected to be at her mother-
in-law's beck and call, but after an overseas sojourn, a daughter-in-

law's obedience is especially tested to see if she has become too selfish. Even in cases where the mother-in-law does not criticize her daughter-in-law, she will still make demands on her time and expect her to visit frequently, even if just for a chat. As one wife said, "In the U.S., I was free of her meddling. She makes me conscious that I live between cultures." Wives of eldest sons, traditionally expected to have the closest contact with their mothers-in-law, can have the hardest time. Several who lived with their mothers-in-law complained that the older woman monopolized the children's attention. One woman felt that the children no longer belonged to her and her husband but had become the grandmother's responsibility. After a long sojourn in the United States, where the nuclear family had become very close, displacement made the woman extremely bitter. In turn, the wives felt that their mothers-in-law were trying to destroy the closeness of their family lives.

In many cases mothers-in-law deprived of their domain of influence during the years when the son's family was away compensate by finding fault with "spoiled" daughters-in-law, who are to them insufficiently filial and ignorant of the kafū, or "family ways."

In some rare cases, however, the relationship changes for the better, and the woman values the friendship of a mother-in-law who has new respect for her daughter-in-law's capabilities and even for her differentness. One woman, for example, won the clear admiration of her mother-in-law who lives next door by asserting new-found differentness. When the family lived in the United States with their two daughters, they enjoyed a typical, happy suburban life, but after returning to Japan, the mother decided to start her own publishing company. At the same time, her family and others began a community project, a seikatsuba (or living center), where neighbors meet on weekends and in the evenings to use communally owned tools and space to make furniture, backyard equipment, and to discuss community plans. They also began a baby-sitting exchange service. Her mother-in-law says their neighborhood is now like a friendly village rather than impersonally urban, and she thanks her daughter-in-law for making it so. The daughter-in-law says that her life overseas, while not in itself radical, helped her by catalyzing what she sees as antiestablishment in herself. She says, "I knew people would think I was strange after returning anyway, so why not do something really strange and useful?" And even she acknowledges that if her children had been boys, she probably would not have launched an unconventional lifestyle in Japan.

Women as Returnees

Although central to the family and crucial to its success and integration in Japanese society, the housewife in the returnee family suffers some constraints on her resourcefulness and power, which reflect the residual quality of the family in Japanese society at large. First, even the most ardent kyoiku mama cannot, by any degree of cajoling and encouraging, ensure that her child will overcome the stigma of a foreign education. Second, however supportive she is of her husband, as in the case of the Fujimuras, his sidetracked career may produce frustration and a sense of inferiority she has no power to ameliorate. Third, her absence from her neighborhood is in itself a problem for her, and total reintegration into her group of friends may be impossible. While her husband (in most cases) still has a circle of returnee friends, and her children may be reasonably happy at an international returnee school, she is usually isolated and may experience a sense of victimization. On the other hand, women who took advantage of the freedom of the overseas experience felt that it was a most important and beneficial catalyst in their lives in Japan. Whether the returnee's time overseas was merely endured or creatively utilized depends *not* on the constraints of membership in an organization, as it did for the husband and children, but on the woman's own motivation and flexibility.

Fathers at Work

Just as a hiatus in education hurts the child's identity as a student and classmate, so absence from the workplace* marks the father as an outsider. The boundaries of the work group are brought into strong relief by the divergent experiences of the returned employee. His identity and skills are called into question, even though he was sent overseas by his company to carry out duties that promote and maintain Japan's highly valued success in the global market. Given the devaluation and stigma attached to those who promote and maintain it, Japan's "internationalization" is in fact remarkably successful.

When faced with the differentness of employees returned from overseas, Japanese companies follow a pattern of exclusion and com-

---

*Although there is a range of workplace types, the discussion here will be restricted to those large firms and government ministries that set the style for a Japanese organization. The words company or firm in this general discussion should be taken to mean a typical large and well-established occupational structure, except where more specific references are given.

partmentalization that resembles what happens in the educational system. By rewarding "normal" background, educational credentials, and uniform work style, and by enforcing a predictable mainstream career path for managers, Japanese organizations make clear distinctions between insiders and outsiders. A Japanese "salary man" (white-collar worker) in a large organization is known by his alma mater, by the company he keeps, and by the style and quality of his work, in that order. For him, a Japanese education, a domestic-focused career path, and a homogeneous and supportive work cohort are the basic elements of predictability and security. His firm, like the educational system, values active, uninterrupted membership.

For large companies and government ministries, *internationalization* has two meanings. The first takes in the structural adjustments made by Japanese institutions to allow for increased and more efficient trade, business negotiations, and deployment of personnel overseas. The second connotes the nebulous area of intercultural communication.

Accordingly, internationalization, as it affects the work of an organization, the deployment of personnel, and the "culture" of Japanese business is seen as both positive and negative. For long-range policy formation by firms and agencies, internationalization is regarded as good. But the phenomenon presents immediate problems for flexible utilization of personnel and thus threatens established patterns of work life and group solidarity.

To understand why internationalization poses a dilemma for the Japanese, I want to address first the issue of how and why an organization establishes its boundaries and then the question of how these are understood and maintained. That is, how does an employee know when he has gone, or been sent, too far? And what devices serve to insulate the firm from the effects of international work? Second, I want to discuss the fit of these limits with the international content of the employee's work. Third, I want to look at how international work is accomplished within the environment of protective accommodation and how the individual worker develops strategies to balance his need to be functionally international with the parochial demands of Japanese group membership. As for the first question, of boundaries, we need to consider the Japanese organization in its domestic setting.

Domestic Work and the Workplace

The normal Japanese workplace and attitudes toward work show patterns of strong differentiation between inside and outside. The domestic organization, even without the more dramatic distinction of domestic versus foreign work, has inherent tendencies toward inclusion and exclusion, which, in turn, color both the work itself and work relationships. But, it should be said, these generalizations pertain to urban, middle-class, college-educated employees. Moreover, we must remember that a distinction exists between career bureaucrats and businessmen on a top management ladder and those whose career paths— determined by credentials, connections, examinations, or personal drive—ends at a middle-management level. This distinction is important in Japan, where the word *career* means a mainstream elite course.[4]

Both terms, *mainstream* and *elite*, are vague but are often used by employees to describe the positions of others in their firms and rarely to describe themselves, except ironically. Since the terms represent an achieved rather than an ascribed track, they usually do not carry the socioeconomic class connotations they may have elsewhere. Individuals, at least ideally, have access through examinations to the mainstream track toward elite positions, and so exclusivity or inaccessibility are not inherent in the term *elite* in Japan. The elite takes in a very small proportion of the working population but represents a model whose characteristics are well understood by most white-collar employees of ministries and the larger corporations. In short, elite jobs are those at the top of the mainstream. And mainstream work moves along a normal advancement path in any large domestic company or ministry. *Mainstream* also implies a general attachment to the organization, while *elite* connotes the vertical power linkages at the upper reaches of the organization. Thus *mainstream* can be applied to any worker in the broad-based pyramid of white-collar jobs in a large company or ministry.

The Meaning of Work

Work, in Japan as elsewhere, is both an economic necessity and a source of personal identity. However, the function of work to give life meaning, what is called *ikigai*, or a reason for living, is particularly strong in Japan. Japanese employees identify more strongly with their workplaces than do their counterparts in any other industrialized country. American employees tend to discard the tasks of the day at five o'clock and seek fulfillment in other activities and contexts. As one Japanese manager in the United States noted, "The Americans work hard, but only from nine to five. They also see themselves as doing a job and . . . that job as their only responsibility."[5] By contrast, the Japanese employee most typically believes that he is defined by his more generalized involvement in his job—an involvement that does not end at the conclusion of the workday but includes time spent at the workplace as well as time spent with colleagues after hours. An American middle-level manager who brings work home or who works overtime is pitied as a workaholic. A Japanese white-collar worker, on the other hand, is expected to work late—several hours past the time when the secretaries leave the office—and to spend his leisure time with his office cohort rather than with family or outside friends.

To be a valued and promotable employee, a Japanese must be what Americans would call a "company man." Although this demands much of the individual's time, it is a comfortable pattern, since tenure and advancement are relatively secure. If a man is patient, he will be advanced in a regular and predictable way. Patience, in fact, is valued above personal initiative, which can be a source of friction, because ambition is regarded as selfishness. As a cohort reaches middle-management level, the leadership positions can go to only a small percentage of the group. Selection for the posts is usually predictable, and at every stage of shrinkage in the pyramid, those who will stay on the leadership ladder have usually known for some time that they would be "chosen." There is a prescribed quality to the advancement patterns, and yet achievement and competition are rewarded. It takes a subtle and sensitive person, like Mr. Kajima, who has spent his time observing the workings of human relations in his office, as well as doing his own work as effectively as he can, to break out of ahead of the pack, sometimes in spite of deficiencies in background or education.

But the opportunities to break ahead are few, and the risks of sticking out are great. In a well-known recruitment ad, Sony—a company known for its nontraditional managerial practices—took issue with the popular saying, "The head that sticks up above the rest gets lopped off," by adding, "We want those heads." But the conventional cautionary aphorism guides more career paths, and Sony is still the exception.

Since work is assigned to a team and not to an individual, the ability to cooperate is vital. Mutuality and a sense of merged work identity are also enforced by the office layout, in which desks face each other and "there is no clear boundary between one person's work and another's.[6] Workmates depend on each other to help with tasks and to cover for each other during sickness and vacations. Although the group is the unit of productivity, the individual still bears great personal responsibility. Each worker must be reliable and consistent, and group cohesion is hurt by the absence of an individual. If a member is absent for a long time, he incurs enormous obligations to his workmates. Even taking one's allotted vacation all at one time is not frequently done. Unlike their American counterparts, most employees take only two or three days off at a time. Japanese employees say that it isn't that there is so much work to do but that one needs to be there to show one's face in the halls *(kao o dasu)* to feel that one belongs. So a two-week family vacation seems inappropriate to the employee and to his work group.

Cohesion and the primacy of the group do not diminish individual responsibility. For the overseas returnee, the restoration of this cohesion represents both his responsibility to the group and an instrumental means for his career development. Thus the diffuse but strongly cohesive Japanese style of task assignment and the patterns of mutuality inherent in workplace groups present great problems for the returnee—he has been absent from the group, and he may have developed a different style of work. He may have vacationed too long.

Recruitment

Recruitment, training, and advancement in many Japanese companies and in most government positions tend to emphasize the creation and reinforcement of diffusely defined but strong bonds between the worker and the institution, rather than selection for or teaching of particular skills. Employees are recruited directly from the university, and some are even signed a year before their graduation. This practice is known as *aotagai,* or "buying rice while it is still green in the paddies." It is assumed that these "betrothed" employees will spend their last year preparing themselves for the style and work of the job they've been promised. But the specific study of one's university days rarely has much to do with the later work of one's job.[7] The most desirable candidates for careers in business and government work are those with liberal arts or law degrees from top-ranking universities, not those with specialized skills in technical areas, no matter how relevant the skill might seem to the work. Being "the right sort of person" is more important than knowing the right things, and companies and ministries prefer to train workers to their own style and type of work after entry.

The link between companies and universities became less overt in 1975, when it was decided not to publicize how many graduates of a particular college entered a particular company or ministry. Still, the connections are strong. Where other factors in a hiring choice are equal, managers and officers give priority to candidates who are recommended by former professors or who belong to their own college clubs. Personnel directors are influenced by the feeling that people work better and more comfortably with each other if there is some kind of prior link. Through such connections the behavior and qualifications of a candidate can be better predicted. More important, they provide preestablished relationships involving obligations and personal networks beyond the job itself. A Japanese employer finds these more important in a new recruit than office and management skills, which are seen as easily acquired on the job by a person whose other qualifications are high.

For the entrant into an organization, the choice is based on the stability of the company and labor conditions. He joins a company because it is solid and well known; he plans to specialize in one aspect of the business; he speaks of moving on or out of the company if advancement and pay raises do not come quickly enough.[8] But the young entrant is quickly assimilated to the norms and values of the company. The personal ties of loyalty that are developed during the orientation period form the basis for his attachment to the company. He exercises his ambition by conforming to the demands of the group.

Training

After joining the company, new employees are not only trained in the work of the organization but are also integrated into a group of their peers—their entering year cohort. It is this group, rather than the office in which he happens to be placed, that cements a person's relation to his company. He relates more intensively and informally with these people than with superiors (or, later, subordinates).[9]

The entry cohort is a logical focus of emotional attachment. Although the employee will change office assignment as frequently as every other year over the span of his work life, the peer group remains constant and relevant. The closeness of this group may be more important even than its productivity: As Robert Bellah notes, "For some groups, integrative values (of the collectivity) have primacy over the goal-attainment values."[10] Although the entry cohort may be torn by conflicts of ambitions at times, it is usually supportive and cohesive. The approval and patronage of superiors is important, but steady teamwork is favored over stellar individual performance in the eyes of both superiors and teammates.

Although the seniority system assures that a worker will be moved up the pay ladder at predictable intervals, achievement or observed talent can push some ahead in status or responsibility. Matters of status and power are handled with much tact, and the compensations of security and equal pay at all levels ensure a minimum of bad feeling among those who might otherwise feel "dropped."[11] Employees of major companies and ministries insist emphatically that their organizations treat them fairly. But their idea of fairness is not based on the idea that individual merit should be rewarded; it depends, initially, on a "maternalistic egalitarianism" that "prescribes equal treatment toward people who have been placed on a given ground and ignores differences in ability or anything else."[12]

How, then, are distinctions made in order to choose employees for advancement? What is valued is a combination of sensitivity to human relationships, observable talents, an appropriate "style," and a strong perceptible loyalty to the organization.[13] Accordingly, many of the requisites for success are hard to define and involve one's relationship to the workplace and workmates more than the meritorious performance of tasks.

Because an employee is trained in the particular skills of his company, and because the security of "permanent employment" creates loyalty, leaving an occupational path is unusual. Most employees enter an organization immediately after graduating from a university, with no break for other training or experience. An employee in a large company or ministry has rarely been employed elsewhere, although mid-career changes are becoming more frequent.[14] In general, an interruption of any sort for any reason is not encouraged.

Family and Work Group

Family and workplace make different and usually complementary claims on an employee's time, offering him separate forms of group membership. The husband focuses on his outside work group; the wife and children, on home and school. The home is a place where the husband can rest and relax and receive emotional support. He in turn provides for the family's welfare and status as a sort of broker to the outside world. While the husband does feel a warm bond with and strong sense of responsibility for his family, he is to some extent regarded as an outsider by the family. Very often his family spends time with him only on Sundays, and his children see him as *nichiyōbi no tomodachi* (a Sunday friend); on other days he leaves the house before they wake and returns after they are in bed. The wife and children consider him of but not in the family, and by subtly excluding him from its daily intimacies they intensify his need to attach himself emotionally to the workplace. Thus his identity is defined by membership in his work group, an identity reinforced by his relationship to his family as a functional or necessary outsider. The employee's family, in other words, gives him a role that in no way conflicts with the demands made on him to give continuous and undivided attention to the company. There is some evidence, however, that at least some Japanese are favoring their families over workplace or career. Especially when it comes to their children's education, family priorities may take precedence over company loyalty. In one such case, a man who had worked for a major electronics company for seventeen years turned down a transfer to Osaka from Tokyo, fearing the effect it would have on his children. He had to quit his company, and he joined an American company to stay in Tokyo—in a real sense sacrificing his own mainstream path in order to maintain his children in the mainstream.

Domestic Generalist versus International Specialist

The generalist-specialist dichotomy is one with a long history in Japan. It has roots in the Chinese scholar-official tradition, in which the most prestigious jobs were characterized by their separation from practical work, which was delegated to clerks.[15] The official's work consisted of upholding the dignity of the office and issuing judgments supported by the language of tradition and authority.

The Japanese manager's or official's major job is not decision making but rather the coordination of tasks, for which he needs a broad and sensitive knowledge of human relations. He is a gentleman-leader whose job it is to maintain harmony and productivity in the sector of the organization under his control. While he must have detailed knowledge of his subordinates' tasks, his own role is formal and not directly instrumental to the specific goals of the organization. Demanding general attributes rather than specialized skills, these jobs are highly sought after, and their titles, such as "director-general," rather than, for example, "director of shipping and transport," denote a status rather than a task.

Those with such status are expected to generate an environment in which employees can work well; the subordinates of the leader work hard out of personal regard for him.[16] In a workplace without a Japanese-style leader, the employee's work will be less tied to his relationship with his superior and more defined by a specific function and measured by his individual productivity. The latter condition would be described by the Japanese as "dry" (bureaucratic) compared to the "wet" (more "human") Japanese arrangement.

The success of personal work remains dependent on team effort. Projects are assigned to a group rather than to individuals, and though specialized skills are used within the group to accomplish the task, individuals having the necessary skills are not usually known beyond the group for these talents. Everyone is trained in specific skills and uses them but is rarely identified with them.

Within an organization vague job definitions and group assignments generate both cohesion and productivity. But the system may break down in negotiations or collaborations with outside or foreign organizations. Inward looking, the arrangement is awkward when dealing with agencies external to it. There is little transferability of the definition and roles of the worker to other organizations—even to other Japanese workplaces.[17] Equally important, there are few roles explicitly designed to bridge the gap between such characteristically Japanese organizations and those of other countries. Moreover, where such "brokers" do exist, as we have seen, they are not considered mainstream employees.

Thus, to some degree, every Japanese group is a separate unit and considers itself a small universe. Strong distinctions between inside and outside govern its interactions, and few formally established structural links exist between these units. On a personal level, too, interaction with others not in one's group is not very well defined, which is evident in the indiscriminate pushing and shoving on subways or the indifference to littering laws in public places. When a link must be established between groups, it is often accomplished through long and remote maneuvering through informal, personal ties—a cousin who knows a manager in Company X will be called and consulted as a kind of go-between for Company Y. Such ties are valued since they provide predictable relationships through the web of preexisting obligations.

That web does exist in domestic Japanese business. But, of course, different strategies have had to emerge to bridge the structural gap in international business; predictability in transcultural personal relationships cannot be assumed. One strategy is the classification of overseas workers as specialist liaison persons. Although it is common practice for international organizations in other countries to have specialized international employees, in the Japanese instance the function and effect of such specialization are quite different.

Very specialized jobs are, in Japan, far from mainstream advancement paths. The segregation by specialization of international liaison employees is an increasingly visible example of a negative distinction. The specialty that these employees are said to possess is not that of an area, such as the Middle East or Europe, or of a particular commodity or task, such as iron ore or shipping, but that of communication itself. And so, it is their tasks of translation, liaison, and contact making that isolate them from the mainstream. These go-between functions are, like generalist tasks in Japan, not directly tied to production; nevertheless, they are negatively assessed in part because they "go between" domestic and foreign organizations and in part because they involve very particular skills. And, since their chief task ties them to a downgraded *function* rather than to generalized work having to do with the internal structure of the firm, they are placed in separate international administrative divisons on a different advancement track, lower in status than the domestic ladder. This occurs even in the Foreign Ministry, where a returnee with very good language skills often becomes a "nonregular staff member *(shokutakujin)* or [is] confined to administrative sections [and] only very infrequently would become a regular career foreign service officer."[18]

Workers who are sent overseas for a two- or three-year posting hope to return to a regular department to avoid the specialist label *kokusaijin* (international person). However, the company anxious to conduct international negotiation and trade with as little basic structural change as possible attempts to use those with specialized experiences in an encapsulated international section. The separation is functional to the organization because the work gets done. It also protects what is seen as an untranslatable pattern of work relationships from the invasion of unfamiliar work values and practices. One of the returnees interviewed, a man who prided himself on being international, said that his firm interprets internationalism as cultural "shiftiness," adding, "My boss wants me to be more bicultural than international—to be a 'hell of a nice guy' in the United States and to bow and hiss in Japan—to switch back and forth as the circumstances require." Thus, foreign ways are to be employed for the good of the organization but *outside* the organization.

Work and Status: Evaluating One's Job

Those on career paths in business and government agencies are of course extremely sensitive to the distinctions between generalist and specialist and domestic and international. From that awareness has emerged a consensus on the "value" of various kinds of work in various combinations in an elite mainstream career.

Domestic Generalists

The most highly valued positions are both domestic and generalist— that is, work is based preferably in the main office and titled by status rather than by skill, whatever the actual work involved. Here are found the large body of ordinary bureaucrats and businessmen whose identities are most strongly tied to workplace and work group. Here also are the jobs of traditional leaders who keep a low personal profile but are adept in the delicacies of human relationships. Mr. Kajima attempts to maintain such a profile at his bank.

There is an important historical dimension in the characterization of present-day business and government leaders as domestic. The top managers are all persons who received most of their education just before and during World War II and who, therefore, were less exposed to international influences than either younger persons just coming into positions of authority or older persons who are now retired or acting as postretirement counselors to their organizations. Very few of the top leaders have had overseas education or experience other than brief trips. Some business leaders feel that after the retirement of this present generation of less internationalized leaders, those with overseas backgrounds will be judged by different standards, and top management positions will be more accessible to internationalized employees. As of the mid-1980s, however, a domestic background is clearly more highly valued than an international one.

International Generalists

The next most valued occupations are international and generalist. These are rare posts, usually held by especially talented persons whose background qualifications (good family connections and degrees from the most prestigious universities) help them avoid the stigma normally attached to an overseas posting. The elite diplomatic posts in such cities as New York, London, Washington, and Bonn and in the top Japanese delegations to international organizations like the International Monetary Fund, the World Bank, or the United Nations are held by such people. Here the officeholder's personal qualifications and connections reinforce the status inherent in the position itself. These elite internationals may of course be sent to other than top posts in the regular recycling of assignments, but they manage to keep their status even in a less-than-desriable posting. The international generalists stress that there are many compensations for not being in Japan: higher pay, better housing, and more time to spend in leisure activities or with their families as well as interesting contacts with foreign counterparts. On the negative side, they realize that no matter how important their overseas role or how good their connections, their children as returnees will be in the same situation as the children of less elite overseas workers. As parents they must make the same difficult choices made by all other returnee parents. They must decide whether to subject their children to the rigors of readjustment to the Japanese educational system or to opt for a temporarily more comfortable international education that at present cannot lead to the most prestigious work or to a mainstream career path. These parents experience a most painful conflict between the ease and excitement of overseas life and the tension of attempting to provide a Japanese future for their children.

Because of their own backgrounds and elite expectations, these parents are among the most vociferous critics of the educational system's treatment of their returnee children. It is this group, with old school ties and family influence, which has put pressure on government and business leaders to fund Japanese education overseas and returnee readjustment schools in Japan.

Domestic Specialists

On the next rung down are the domestic specialists, who are employees of large companies or ministries. They have usually passed a "Class II" entrance examination and so are not on a so-called career path. Accountants, salesmen, research specialists in fuel, raw materials, and so on and people with high clerical or administrative posts all fall into this category. Although sometimes considered anonymous and boring, such jobs are at least located in Japan, where loyalty and hard work produce a predictable security and a strong sense of identity.[19]

International Specialists

International specialists occupy the least valued positions. This category includes translators, area specialists, and overseas agricultural or mining technicians and advisers—anyone known by his or her communications skills or by a geographical area rather than by an organization on which he or she can rely for security and identification. This group of overseas employees is the most rapidly growing; the great increase in overseas branches, offices, plants, and technical or other information-gathering agencies has necessitated the development of specializations among employees.

At the same time, a need to economize has lengthened overseas stays in such posts, which also increases the likelihood that these employees will develop speciality skills. Unless they develop a "loner" strategy—in which they can derive satisfaction from the very aspects of their work that deny them "normal" Japanese identities—they may be the most unhappily isolated of the internationals. Their skills are usually not applicable to domestic work, and in the case of interpreters, there is much prejudice against their craft. One of the mothers in the sample of returnees, lamenting about the choice of jobs she felt were open to her son in Japan, said, "I'd rather he were a garbage man than an interpreter." Her comment, an extreme reaction to international specialization, nonetheless points to the general problem of the adaptability of the Japanese definition of work in new contexts. (The job of interpreter is perhaps a special case, since it is seen as merely a go-between job with no direct ties to a work team. Go-betweens are prevalent in domestic environments, but they are not stigmatized by their role, probably because their duties do not include negotiations between very different contexts and the use of other—non-Japanese—skills.)

The Hayashis, Kajimas, and Fujimuras belong to three different occupational groups: academic, banking, and the government bureaucracy. (Descriptions of international work in other types of organizations are offered in appendix 4.) How were their returns to Japan affected by the kinds of jobs the fathers have?

Like many Japanese academics who conduct research or teach overseas, Professor Hayashi did so on his own initiative. Although there is some flexibility and freedom in being a university teacher, the structure of even the most experimental new university is similar to the seniority-based, vertical organization of a traditional firm, and absence from the structure of relationships in an academic department can be as dangerous to a career as absence from the company—especially when the absence is self-initiated.

In the traditional "chair system" of a Japanese university, a professor has a constellation of assistants around him who depend on him for advancement and for introductions to his colleagues.[20] To receive the benefits of this relationship, the disciples must be attentive and stay close to their teacher; they maintain the relationship even after receiving their own faculty appointments.[21] Time and effort must also be devoted to maintaining collegial relationships, and Professor Hayashi complained of the load of "glue work"—the administrative and committee work that hold the group together.

In a university the young must work hard to be acceptable, while the older are given a bit more freedom to explore and diversify. Thus, an overseas sojourn is more problematic the younger one is. Informants said that if one spends even a year or two abroad before receiving a permanent appointment, one may as well give up the idea of university work in Japan except at an international college. After a professor finds a post for his student, and the new appointee spends a few years making his own niche, it is then possible for him to leave for a year of "enrichment" overseas, but the longer he waits before going, the better his chances for a smooth reentry. The tenuously established returnee must rely almost exclusively on his teacher's benevolence, which may have been sorely tested by his absence.

It is rare to find an academic returnee who has not also experienced at least some discomfort with his teacher and colleagues. Overseas he will either have worked independently as a researcher on his own project or as part of a research team at a foreign university, and he will have grown used to independence and to patterns of cooperation different from those of his home university. The rigid hierarchy of a Japanese department will in many cases come as something of a shock to the returnee, who will be considered a subordinate of his former teacher and who often does not feel comfortable returning to a subservient role. An extreme and tragic example of such a strained relationship was reported in 1976, when an assistant professor who, scolded by his superior for speaking before him at an international conference, committed suicide. In his diary he wrote that he could not aspire to promotion any longer, since he had insulted his superior. He blamed his inability to control himself on his life overseas.[22] Even where such a strong and crucial relationship does not exist, there are often still problems with colleagues who can bring strong pressure to bear. Professor Hayashi was strongly criticized for both of his postdoctoral stays overseas on the grounds that he was ignoring the needs of the group and that others would be inconvenienced by his absences. In the university *international* is sometimes equated with *selfish*.

Thus, because of problems with reentry into hierarchical relationships and because of difficulty in reassimilating to a group of colleagues, returnees often have problems with their academic careers. Many claimed that they were given no chance by their superiors or their peers to prove their loyalty to their department and were treated as contaminated. As Professor Hayashi commented, "Either one is a pure Japanese or an impure international—my colleagues think the overseas experience has dirtied me—or they are envious!" Because of such group pressure, those with international experiences feel they must play down their past. For example, one professor said, "If you've been overseas and inadvertently say to a colleague, 'When I was in Chicago," you must catch yourself quickly and add, 'I had a terrible time.'" There are some cases of international typing in the academic context that mirror the plight of a specialist in a firm. Some departments may informally designate one man as the department's regular "ambassador" to overseas conferences rather than distributing the duty (or pleasure) among the faculty. Those with an academic specialization in overseas areas are of course particularly appropriate for the designation.

To summarize: For the academic the overseas sojourn has minimal career effect if the person is well established in his or her profession and is willing to meet the demands of departmental relations. However, because many top-ranking university departments are very traditional, it is sometimes impossible for a returnee academic, especially those in junior positions, to reintegrate him- or herself into the social structure of the organization.

Mr. Kajima returned to his bank in Tokyo and experienced relatively little displacement, but he had laid his groundwork well.

In recent years banking in Japan has become increasingly international. Banks differ, of course, in the amount of foreign business they do, and in banks where little is done, overseas work can be a disadvantage to one's career, since it is off the normal path. However, in banks that do more, there is less stigma attached to a temporary overseas post or in an assignment to the international desk at home. Going abroad is not in itself considered to devalue the worker, and in fact it is glamorous and interesting to many younger employees. While banking, like government work, derives its identity from a domestic focus, banks are in the business of capital accumulation and development, rather than that of the preservation and representation of Japanese values and institutions. Unlike government work, then, banking needs to be more open to diverse influences and more flexible in its approach to the external environment. However, in its domestic orientation, banking still offers very little by way of international career opportunities for employees. In fact, when an international section becomes more significant in the overall work of a bank, a domestic manager is often put in charge of it. This can damage the morale of the international employees, who may sometimes resign. While bankers say that it is good to have *some* exposure to international work, the criteria for advancement remain domestic: good business competence and the ability to work well with others as well as a range of experiences across the bank's sectors. Mr. Kajima said that bank personnel managers believe that if an employee is good at languages, he is probably not good at banking.

As for methods of recruitment and work style, there are few differences between a career in a domestically centered bank and a career in an elite domestic ministry. In a typical large bank, twenty five to thirty five top university graduates enter the career path each year. After several years (sometimes as many as five) in training, a few will be selected for training in overseas universities, and after that a few of these will be assigned to overseas posts. These few are considered to be the best of their group, and their sojourns abroad are a kind of grooming for future top assignments at home.[23]

Overseas work, done at the right time (early) and in the right places (New York, London, Paris, Frankfurt, or Hong Kong) can aid advancement or be a sign that one is advanceable. In one large Tokyo-based bank, 80 percent of domestic department heads and all the heads of the international divisions had had overseas assignments early in their careers. Now, however, for straight-line advancement, employees at the level of section chief and above must be domestic in their recent experience. The present top managers had had overseas assignments when young, in a period when such posts were seen as less damaging.

The dangers of overseas postings for bankers are similar to the dangers in other careers. Some overseas postings may indicate that one has been "gotten out of the way." But, as in other professions, one

cannot tell from the posting alone, since the value of a banking assignment varies in a kind of rough cycle. Some overseas assignments are
for a while regarded as prestigious and are therefore filled by a succes-
sion of persons on a top management track. If, however, the position
is devalued for some reason, those who subsequently fill it are perceived as unsuccessful. The shifts in status seem to be determined
more by internal, home office politics than they are by the nature of
the work or place overseas. In one bank, for example, Johannesburg
had been a very good assignment, actively sought by employees. However, a branch manager there became involved in a fight in the home
office, and he was kept in South Africa much longer than the term of
a standard posting. The post subsequently became a symbol for exile
even for those who came after him.

After an overseas assignment, an employee returns to an international division, no matter what his work was before the posting.[24] This
is seen partly as an efficient use of skills acquired overseas and partly
as a way to guarantee work to people who have acquired differentness
of work style or personality in an overseas posting and who thus might
present problems in a domestic job. One observer has noted that bankers who have worked overseas *can* be "laundered" if they "stay clean"
for eight years. As of the current writing, Mr. Kajima has been eleven
years without a long-term overseas post and has instead a "frequent
flyer" position, in which he travels often for periods no longer than a
week. He feels quite safe.

Mr. Fujimura has borne the brunt of both chance and choice in his
career with his ministry. He had no plan to attempt a "pure path" and
in fact had *sought* international work. But overseas work wtih an
explicit tie to an international organization and the repeated overseas
sojourns put him on a path whose image he hadn't expected.

International work in the Foreign Ministry is, ambitious employees
would say, twice cursed. The ministry itself is said to be merely
Japan's "doorman," maintaining lines of communications so that others can step in to do the real negotiating. While many Foreign Ministry employees, especially those attached to top bureaus such as the
North American section, are excellent linguists and career-track elit-
ists, their positions depend more on their educational backgrounds and
their overall (generalist) skills than on their linguistic talents.

Everywhere, diplomacy has long been considered an elite occupation practiced by well-educated men with good connections and broad
vision. The special gifts these men possess, such as skill in languages
and an ability to move easily in foreign societies, have to some degree

lost their cachet in Japan, and while they remain extremely important to the ministry, these skills are no longer so deliberately cultivated by individuals. Elite work in the Foreign Ministry has turned to domestic, bureaucratic concerns. One result of the shift is that the Japanese diplomat abroad no longer has the freedom or power to negotiate or make decisions. Foreign policy has in fact become strongly tied to domestic economic concerns, and much of the actual negotiation on behalf of Japan is done by other ministries, among them the Ministry of International Trade and Industry (MITI), or by the trading companies in the course of their overseas transactions.

To make its image more attractive to prospective elite applicants, the Foreign Ministry tries to equalize postings by spreading undesirable ones over a larger group of people. One of the strategies recently adopted involves removing the stringent language requirements for entrance. Dictation and conversation tests were dropped in 1976, leaving only a short translation and composition test, with the hope of attracting "potential good diplomats" from the most prestigious departments of the best universities. These candidates, it was felt, would be neither linguists nor adventurers but generalist career persons. By training candidates in languages after entrance to the ministry, the personnel office feels it has a wider and more qualified pool of persons with mainstream intentions from which to choose.

Even in the Foreign Ministry, overseas work can make one offtrack. "Remote control" in the case of the Foreign Ministry means that all control and decision making emanates from Tokyo. Even ambassadors feel that their experience and advice counts for little, even in making local decisions in their own posts. For example, a recent ambassador to the Netherlands, when informed of the emperor's upcoming trip to Europe, urged strongly that the trip not include Holland, where he knew there was much anti-Hirohito feeling, because he wanted to avoid an embarrassing scene. The Foreign Ministry ignored his advice, and the emperor's entourage endured a demonstration and was pelted with eggs and ketchup. Afterward the Japanese press blamed the Japanese embassy for its insensitivity to local conditions. Similarly, overseas research and information offices find that any proposals generated in their offices are thoroughly screened and, without a lot of lobbying in Tokyo, generally fail; whereas all proposals emanating from Tokyo are carried out without question.

The work of many lower-level appointments in the Foreign Ministry and other ministries with overseas posts attached to embassies consists only in *atendo* (attendant) duties as guides and interpreters for visiting task-force teams sent from Japan. This work, smoothing the path for negotiations, is often difficult, but it is felt to be only a service job.

Employees and even career diplomats in the United States Foreign Service express similar feelings about their work overseas, but without the same conviction that domestic work based in Washington would be better. Also, since they are much freer to find satisfying work outside and often in fact plan to work in the private sector after a term or two in the foreign service, they are not as dependent on their organization.

Like other Japanese ministries and businesses, the Foreign Ministry is oriented to a domestic style and connections, and career employees work hard to maintain a home-office stance. Although in theory advancement is equitable and "rational," a feeling prevails that one must engage in a struggle for recognition by being in Tokyo as much as possible. Only here can one show one's work and abilities to one's superiors and secure better postings. Even two consecutive Washington postings without home leave have been known to make career diplomats anxious. Because employees believe that they have little structured control over the directions of their careers, they rely on constant attendance, symbolic gestures, and informal personal attentions to further their cause.

There is a high degree of consensus as to which Foreign Ministry posts are the most desirable for elite, career-track diplomats: Washington, Paris, New York, Bonn, and London. A sojourn at one of these in the first five or six years of one's career enhances later elite advancement, according to officials. Many more postings have been established now in developing countries, especially in places where valuable natural resources are available, such as OPEC nations. Although these posts pay about fifty percent more than posts in Washington, they are not considered desirable assignments. They are often given as second postings to employees who are already overseas and who thus have less leverage with which to get better posts. Those career diplomats who are sent to developing countries are usually younger (twenty-five to thirty-five), since, for both institutional and personal reasons, it is not desirable to post older men to such places.

The overseas experience is intrinsic to the work of the Foreign Ministry, so there is no separate section for returnees equivalent to the international desk of a company or the International Bureau in the Finance Ministry. However, since there is still a preference for and a focus on the activities of the domestic as opposed to the foreign workplace, the Foreign Ministry's strategy is to avoid, by constant recycling of posts, typing employees as international. Personnel directors claim that these frequent shifts help preserve the unspecialized flexibility wanted in a career diplomat. It is also said that the unspecialized generalist worker is best suited to the biennial change of jobs. From the employee's point of view, it is best to be a generalist doing domestic work, and so those on a career path are often at least as interested in what is happening in Tokyo as in developments in their overseas posting.

Leadership roles in the Foreign Ministry continue to demand a generalist approach in which knowledge of human relations and a broad overview of the ministry's work remain the acknowledged attributes of leadership. Since leadership demands such hard-to-define skills, more specialized duties fall to the younger and lower-ranking foreign service officers. While it frequently happens that a high official has a period of international-specialist work in his past, ambitious young men now avoid such work in their desire to be marked as leadership material from the start.

Older men have remarked that the impatience of the young men to rise to top positions, instead of waiting their turn learning a variety of tasks, has made them model themselves after the generalist leaders prematurely, which their elders see as ludicrous or impertinent. Ambition may have made some younger men more conservative and eager to avoid international work. It is paradoxical that young officers feel that only those who deliberately avoid the stigma of internationalization can rise to the top in the ministry that most depends on effectiveness in the world abroad.

The resistance to internationalization in both domestic and international ministries is tied to a generally conservative mind-set and a traditional focus on internal domestic affairs. It is also tied to the structure of the organization that is based on strong personal bonds and to work style that is rooted in constant and dependable group effort. No less than in domestically based ministries, absence itself threatens group and interpersonal cohesion, and returnees introduce differentness into a system that relies on homogeneity. Because of his personal background, his multiple postings, and his lack of control over his work image, Mr. Fujimura sees himself as not twice but thrice cursed.

Strategies of Return

As we have seen, personal strategy seems to play some part in successful reentry. By looking at the variety of choices and chances represented in my sample, we may see to what extent an individual can determine the course of things. Three main types of strategy were easily discernible among the informants. They are: reassimilators, adjusters, and internationals.[25] All three groups have nearly the same view of Japanese society and the occupational system. They all believe that the Japanese group is a demanding environment with a strong distinction between outside and inside. Since they all, to some degree, saw themselves as outsiders, they have had to develop conscious strategies: to try to reassimilate into their group as decontaminated insiders; to adjust their cosmopolitanism to a more domestic style while accepting a somewhat marginal position in their firm; or, in the case of the internationals, to become permanent outsiders—actively seeking or passively accepting the role of international outsider. Data concerning characteristics of the sample and strategies of return are presented in appendix 3.

REASSIMILATORS

Reassimilators attempt to erase signs of the overseas sojourn by avoiding markedly foreign clothing, habits, or language. Although young people in Japan today universally wear clothing virtually indistinguishable from that of modern urban societies in the West, and no one considers Western fashion "nonJapanese," a reassimilator has to be careful to wear the same dark suit, white shirt, and black shoes that his office mates wear. If *his* tie is a little wider, or *his* hair a little longer, it will be attributed to his overseas stay and not to an interest in more with-it fashions. In many cases, the assimilating returnee will try to be *plus japonais que les japonais* in his effort to be pure.

Reassimilators were often hard to locate because of a perceived need to "cover" their overseas experience. Thus they are not as available through a network of returnees, since they often deliberately avoid associating with others, Japanese or foreign, from overseas. The following case is typical: I once went to interview an employee of an important ministry who had received a degree at a Midwestern university in the United States. I was to meet him at the gate, but since I was early and knew his office number, I thought I would save him trouble and went upstairs. Opening the door, I saw the usual rows of desks facing each other, the usual shirtsleeved men, younger ones near the front of the room, older ones at the sides and at more imposing desks. But before I could take a step in, I was whisked out of the office and into an empty conference room by a man in a dark blue suit, white shirt, and polished black shoes. He had been terrified when he saw me, he told me later, and had quite intentionally asked me to meet him downstairs, lest the others see me and be reminded of his former apostasy. He also said he was careful not to sprinkle his talk with English, careful to dress conservatively—some returnees wear colored shirts and light-colored ties—and he never mentioned his overseas stay to his coworkers.

ADJUSTERS

Some of those in the adjuster group seem, except for their willingness to talk freely of their experiences and their maintenance of contacts with other returnees, to be very similar in occupation and style to the reassimilators.

Like the students in another study, a person in this group "takes his Japanese identity for granted; it is not a focus of personal concern or reevaluation."[26] He traverses a Japanese career easily, since he returns to the company, ministry, or university from which he came.

Adjusters in general are more relaxed or more passive in their approach to the demands of Japanese society. They try to demonstrate their eagerness to work hard for the firm but are willing to take on some liaison or other sidetracked roles if placed in those positions. They avoid talking about overseas life and try to restore themselves to coffeehouse and bar-group intimacy but tend not to concentrate so narrowly on the struggle to retain a place on the highest promotional path.

INTERNATIONALS

The internationals accept and exhibit their differentness. Unlike adjusters, they may deliberately seek change, either for more flexibility in work style or for a better job. People who fall in this group make a subtle calculation. Persons who feel that the facts of their overseas life (such as a very long stay abroad or one in a low-status location) make it hard for them to be accepted as ordinary employees may decide to exploit their internationalism by marketing themselves within their companies as translators or liaison persons. They may even create such jobs for themselves. Of course, in most firms there is little choice of job assignments, but a person who emphasizes this language or communications skills will find himself doing international work.

A case of this sort is that of Mr. A., who lived overseas for fifteen years and who now works as an executive in heavy industry. He has chosen to work in a mainstream organization with which he had had strong personal connections but no previous employment before he returned to Japan. However, he says that he would not have been hired if he had not chosen to be an international. He is a happy "black sheep" who does not hide his previous experience but rather flaunts it. He sees it as a mechanism for achieving a kind of freedom and is not interested in the tight-knit groups of the normal mainstream. He associates mostly with other internationals and with foreigners, for an American company has a 15 percent interest in his company. He functions as a liaison to the outside and knows that this company needs people like him, who are direct and frank, to communicate between divisions. He feels he can take shortcuts in the vertical communications networks and speed up internal negotiations since he is known for his "American" directness and since he is used to the American style of instant horizontal communications. He feels lucky: He has benefited from and utilized his international style and is confident that he will remain secure in his unusual job. He says that he would not have done so well if he had tried to be "normal."

The internationals fall in two groups. The first group includes very highly motivated persons with an elite background who surmount the hazards of internationalism and are accepted in mainstream occupations, though with an almost "celebrity" visibility. Persons in this group often have parents or grandparents who were international in a period when such a role was prestigious, or they are themselves older people of the self-made elite type of a generation ago.

The second group includes younger people who, impatient with the slow pace of Japanese career advancement and with the style of work life in Japanese offices, have chosen employment either in foreign-owned firms or universities or in nontraditional arts and media. These may be called "international dropouts." Not all in this group have *chosen* to be internationals. Those who spent many years overseas either in advanced training or working for a foreign company, and who returned to Japan either for personal reasons or because they were laid off overseas, now find themselves nearly unemployable in Japanese companies. They must either use their (now weak) network of family and school connections to find work at a lower income and status level than they have been used to or work as translators or liaisons in foreign firms. They are treated, they say, like foreign-born Japanese, a particularly déclassé kind of "foreigner" in Japan.

Many (74 percent) of the women interviewed who had worked overseas were internationals of the second type. This may be because many families feel that girls can afford to be international. However, the women in the group also say that the kind of work they do allows them to have more control over their lives, to have better advancement potential, and to express themselves more fully than work in the mainstream. But female career employees, whether domestic or international, are rare, and most full-time women professionals are considered marginal anyway.

Though the internationals are varied in their motivations and paths, I have grouped them together since, for employers and the wider society, these people seem to be outsiders—the latter group irreparably so and the former saved by a combination of ascribed status, ambition, and talent.

A great variety of prior experiences may have influenced the paths of the "international dropouts." Early "differentness," sometimes first experienced in childhood, led to an offtrack career in several cases. Others, like Mr. Fujimura, reported incapacitating illnesses that kept them at home for more than a year during adolescence, and they date their feelings of separateness from that time. Sickness for them meant isolation rather than discomfort or incapacity, and they became introspective and individualistic. They also reported a kind of "conversion" experience during illness, which they believed made them more self-reliant and less tied to the roles and traditions of Japanese group life.

Many of the "international dropouts" who work for foreign companies chose their path during the Occupation, when they thought that their futures would be most secure with American institutions. Several went to the United States to study and work. One of them returned after thirteen years to find that he had made an error in prediction: Postwar Westernization had not extended to occupational style, and a domestic focus was after all much more important than his international skills.

In short, internationals are usually very elite or very eccentric. Returnees who fall in between have to try somehow to reassimilate or adjust and do so with some hope of success. Ordinary returnees do some of both, yet most do not ordinarily see themselves developing explicit and active strategies. Although they fall into one or another of the modes described above, for most, what they do might better be called "coping."

6

Can They Go Home Again? Brokers and Borders in Modern Japan

Japan's desire to protect and maintain its unique, homogeneous, and closed island identity is rivaled only by its desire for full-scale involvement and success in the world economy. The paradox of an international Japan—a nation of both cultural isolation and international exchange—is not just a fascinating if academic irony. Real human beings—the returnees—shoulder the burden of the paradox. Their perceived impurity leads to their segregation from mainstream education and work. Their transgression across Japan's geographical borders, as essential as it is to Japan's economic success, calls into question their Japanese identity.

The Returnee and Group Identity

We observed employees in companies, children in schools, and housewives in the family and community. We have examined the experience of the returnee and contrasted it to the mainstream Japanese experience, in which people find unambiguous support, security, and identity in school, work, and family.

School, work, and family are primary groups—basic social environments with clear demands on their members. Lines of loyalty are clearly drawn. The employee is loyal to his work team and his company. The child, engaged in the goals of his elders, prepares for occupational success. The mother supports her husband and children and accepts the primacy of their duties and identities as students and employees.

When an individual leaves the domestic group to perform international duties, strains are placed on both the group and the individual. The marginal returnee in a company may find his work compartmentalized to ensure the maintenance of a "pure" Japanese organization. Such a person may be placed in a "waiting post," with few or no real tasks, until an appropriate position opens—or until retirement. He may be placed in an international section, where he continues to do liaison tasks—translation, guiding foreign guests, or travel. He may be sent to a branch office in the hinterlands.

Similarly, the educational system tries to reintegrate those students who are only slightly out of step and relegates others to nonmainstream schools to avoid heterogeneous confusion in the regular system. Children may be first "reprocessed" through a counseling system that judges the level of readjustment education necessary and then placed in readjustment classes, special schools, or international schools that separate them from their more domestic peers and that may prevent them from having a mainstream Japanese career. There is much ambiguity over the educational value of the international experience and parallel ambivalent attitudes toward the returnees: They are seen either as troublesome agents of discord or as helpless victims. In reaction, employees develop various strategies of compliance, adjustment, or rebellion to deal with the sidetracking and outsider status that accompany overseas assignments and the return to Japan.

Mothers may respond similarly to pressures from their communities, but their roles are less institutionalized. In their neighborhoods and circles of friends and kin they are suspect, and their behavior is closely watched. They may have trouble reentering social groups and maintaining relationships with friends. Any sign of differentness will be negatively ascribed to their "foreignness." After experiencing family intimacy overseas, they may feel excluded from their husbands' lives in Japan. The responsibility for their children's education and future will seem especially burdensome after shared responsibility overseas. Further, they must continue to provide nurturing support for their husbands and children who face frustration and difficulties outside the home.

The children themselves must develop strategies similar to those of their parents. However, because the educational system places the greatest pressure on them to conform and because educational credentials are the single most important guarantee of a successful life, returnee children make their choices under powerful external influences. They cannot help but feel that their whole future depends on being "as Japanese as possible," although they are all too aware that they are already marked as different.

We have seen that the stigma and isolation experienced by returnees and their families cannot be explained solely in concrete functional terms. Those with international experience clearly have not totally forgotten the skills needed, such as language, to be Japanese. For the most part they are *functionally* able to resume Japanese life. Thus, their disability on their return seems to stem from a *perceived* tainting or disloyalty. I now want to turn to what it means to be a member of the uchi of Japanese society and will explore some reasons why Japan ascribes such importance to boundary crossing.

The Japanese Concept of Boundary

We have seen that when Japanese travel abroad they cross not only a geographical border but also a social boundary. To do so is to violate the often unspoken rules that define membership.[1] Group membership in general may have primarily political or contractual dimensions (expressed in ideological terms, whether those of religion, business, or politics); it may be marked, as in some ethnic groups, by common rituals and sentiments; or it may be measured by active participation and constant interaction with other members. Each type of membership has a different checklist or qualifications by which the boundary is defined.[2] For my purposes I will call the criteria of membership "contract," "commonality," and "relationship."

The boundary crossed by Japanese returnees—their transgressions, in fact—is defined by criteria marking the importance of relationships. Membership in a Japanese group is mandated not by a particular contract, behavior, or belief but by active presence and participation in the social network—a constant maintenance of the predictable obligations and interactions that make up group membership.[3] The goal of participation is not a product but a process—a process of teamwork, of balancing individual achievement and group harmony in the school, and of planning and support at home. Thus, membership can never be totally assumed; it is not embodied in a contract or in citizenship papers that can be carried on one's person. Belonging does not just depend on active involvement, it *is* that daily interaction itself, and there is no acceptable substitute for being there. Accordingly, the Japanese concept of mothering rejects the idea of substitutes such as baby-sitters. Similarly, career paths are not likely to be held open for those who leave. And in the schools there is great concern about the extended absence of children—concern not simply about whether children can stay on a rigidly defined educational track leading toward competitive and uniquely Japanese examinations but also about their ability to maintain Japanese ways as students—cooperative, engageable, and devoted to achievement. For mothers, fathers, and children alike, it is as though they were being graded on attendance first, performance second.

When Japanese leave Japan, their membership is suspended. Every year they are away, reentry as members of the group—reestablishment of relationships to the satisfaction of those at home—becomes more difficult. It is particularly difficult if after reentry they betray their exposure to foreign ways, which reminds others of the severing of bonds. Reentry raises questions of identity that can be silenced only by strict conformity and virtual denial of the foreign experience.

The strictness with which Japanese boundaries are laid down stems in part from a long cultural tradition of inside-outside distinctions surrounding the uses of space and the demarcation of borders. The central image is that of the home—its private and public spaces. Japanese are socialized in early childhood to differences between inside and outside, between "our house" and others—to the notion of the kafū, a family's own way of doing things—the near-taboo against entertaining nonintimate friends at home. The genkan (entrance hall), where one removes one's shoes, guards the purity of the inside from the pollution of the outside. And children are taught to avoid the edges of tatami floor matting and not to step on the wooden beams that mark doorways.

This conditioning in domestic symbolism adds force to boundaries confronted later in life. But social boundaries in Japan go beyond symbolic ritual and are based in a fundamental concern with interpersonal interactions. New members, whether infants or workplace recruits, are socialized to the group's specific rules for interaction. The most important of these deals not with the quality but rather the quantity of interaction. Members learn that they must be predictably and constantly attentive to relationships with others. When such a group also defines proper membership in terms of observation of rules and filiality, hierarchical patterns, or general predictability of behavior, little is left undefined by the criteria for belonging.

The home is a powerful reference point, and the family—especially the norms of the traditional family—still guides and shapes wider arenas and the expectations of individuals. The reciprocity of interdependent relationships outside the family is directly based on the amae (dependency seeking) of the parent-child relationship.[4] The responsibilities and benefits of hierarchical relationships, the assumptions of generative support and security, and the predictability of an individual's commitment and productivity all come directly out of family-based norms. Even as the actual family unit has diminished in scale and scope, family-style membership has waxed in workplace and school, and it may even be said that under pressures to internationalize, Japan itself has become a macro-uchi. Thus, the boundaries crossed by returnees may well be symbolized by the wooden beam of the doorway and the genkan where one leaves one's shoes.

In a traditional rural village one can clearly see the norms of Japanese group membership that lead to the exclusion or stigmatization of those who ignore the necessary face-to-face relationships and of those who also cross prohibited boundaries. The small, fixed community of an agricultural village was both geographically distinct and socially homogeneous, and its cohesion was based on shared tasks demanding the cooperation of all households. Acts that threatened the relationships integrating a hamlet were a clear violation of group norms and in extreme cases were punished by ostracism. If, for instance, a person passed over the hamlet committee and took grievances to outside legal or political institutions, the group boundaries would have been crossed and its internal problems exposed to the outside world. This was regarded as a breakdown of village cohesion. Typical punishment was to make the offender the hamlet messenger—a go-between role shunned by others.[5]

Although many writers see group sanctions as pressure to conform, I regard the Japanese group as demanding social cohesion primarily through *active* relationships rather than through individual conformity to explicit and fixed behavioral and cultural norms. Thus, eccentricity and individual self-expression were not in themselves abhorred in a traditional village, while willful isolation or withdrawal from relationships and group activities was.

The pressure on a returnee to demonstrate his identity may appear to be pressure to conform to prescribed traits, but even the most assiduous reassimilator's difficulty in being accepted illustrates that it is not conformity alone that counts. To understand better the nature of the boundary crossed by returnees, I will contrast the Japanese boundary defined by relationship to others defined by contract and commonality. Then, to highlight the boundary most painfully violated by returnees—that of the occupational group—I will contrast that group to other Japanese groups.

Groups defined by contract suffer little from external relationships because the group will tend to define those relationships in the same concrete, contractual terms in which internal membership is defined. Such a group would defend its boundaries only when contracts are violated. For example, in an agricultural cooperative, a farmer who refused to put in work time might be denied membership, a food processor caught trying to buy crops from members privately might be publicly denounced, and those members secretly selling on the side might be excluded or severely reprimanded. Such behavior would constitute a breach of contract.

On the other hand, a unit like an American high school clique strongly resembles the Japanese group: Based on relationship, it has fewer contractual and fewer institutionalized rules of membership. In both groups, membership depends on constant interaction and a conformity that is finely tuned to changing practices and fads; a high school clique may exclude a member for simply not wearing a fashion that is in favor with the others or for displaying an aberrant taste in classical music. But more important to the clique is active participation; if a member spends too much time in the company of nonmembers, she will be excluded. The agricultural cooperative requires attention to a "rationally"determined set of criteria based on mutual economic benefit. The high school clique, like the Japanese group, is bound together by the myriad aspects of cohesion and interaction manifested in a conformity that may be said to be both the determinant of membership and the active, changing goal of the group. In other words, cohesion and interaction themselves become the goal.

Members of groups defined by commonality are potentially more defensive than members of those based on contract but less defensive than members of those based on relationships. Membership is available to any who express common beliefs or claim common heritage. Some exchange with the outside is possible; even in ethnically defined groups, some outsiders may acquire commonality by "conversion" and be accepted. While there may be a strong sense of opposition to those not sharing the common belief, heritage, or behavior, these do not pervade all aspects of life nor do they require constant interaction and maintenance.

For example, an American civil rights activist group is defined by shared beliefs, principles, and forms of activity (marches, speeches, boycotts, and so on.) Within the group some members may judge others to be more or less committed. But for the group there are no strict rules of entry or of reentry following a period of inactivity. While the common political beliefs that define the group may carry with them certain preferred styles of relating (for example, egalitarian versus elitist), group members accept major differences of time commitment, background, family situation, and life-style among themselves. Japanese employees, by contrast, share reliance on other predictable social structures (notably the schools and the family) for their preparation and unconflicted support. Thus, the Japanese work group not only requires more constant and active participation than the civil rights organization, but that active participation presupposes embeddedness in other highly ordered and stable social structures. The criteria for Japanese occupational membership are much more pervasive than the criteria typical of political, ethnic, family, or religious groups in the United States.

Members of each type of group interact differently with nonmembers, depending on how threatening interaction is presumed to be. External contact or influence in the agricultural cooperative does not usually threaten membership per se, unless it stands in the way of the group's economic goals. The external activities of the civil rights worker are only threatening if they clearly contradict the basic beliefs of the group; for example, if an activity betrays acceptance of racism. For the Japanese group and the high school clique, in both of which the goal of the group is the face-to-face interaction itself, external relationships are almost always seen as potentially threatening. For instance, in the high school clique, the group fantasies that help it cohere and conform may center on heterosexual romance. But if a member has a real-life boyfriend who takes more of her time than she gives to the group, her loyalty to the group comes into question. She is not, of course, breaking any explicit group law. In fact, she is behaving successfully, given the values of the group. However, her absence and consequent lack of interaction with other members are more a problem for the group than is out-and-out nonconformity to group values.

The most heavily defended type of group seems to be the one based on relationships in which constant and well-choreographed interactions determine a person's identity within it. Conformity or close adherence to detailed rules in everyday relationships is not the group's goal but acts as a defense against outsiders. Such a group is characterized by a strong perception of threat, well-defended external boundaries, and restrictive membership criteria. In fact, the more "active" the criteria of membership in such a group, the more difficult it is for a member to participate in the outside world without threatening his group identity. In other words, criteria of belonging that emphasize relationships between members and that prescribe specifically the manner of relating tend to define any activity outside the group as nonparticipation. On the other hand, groups in which membership is defined by occasional participation, observance of group rites, or celebrations or by paying taxes and obeying laws can tolerate personal "differentness," unconventional relationships, or multiple memberships in other entities.[6]

Is It Enough to Be "Ethnic"?

Although membership by relationship may coincide with racial, religious, or other ideological commitments and identities, it would be a mistake to attribute Japanese cohesion and protectiveness to Japanese culture in the sense of ethnicity. Ethnic traits do not have the same cohesive power in every society. While the French take great pride in their language, food, and art as denominators of cultural identity and may defend their identity with purity-the-language campaigns and gustatorial chauvinism, the Japanese freely indulge in hamburgers and lace their language with words derived from Portuguese, French, German, and English, making it a living record of waves of cultural contact. For the Japanese, social rather than cultural identity is most salient and most defended.

The simplest definition of being Japanese is to be born in Japan, to be of Japanese parents, to live in Japan, and to speak Japanese. As we have seen, a person is Japanese not only because he or she speaks Japanese, likes raw fish, and carries a Japanese passport, but because he or she is an active participant in relationships with clearly drawn lines of responsibility and loyalty.[7] These relationships are embedded primarily in the workplace, the school, and the family, three social structures that operate efficiently in a complementary relationship with each other to make Japan a model of economic growth and success. Thus, while in the lives of the returnees the social demands of being Japanese conflict with the economic demands of a strong "international" Japan, it is those same demanding and rigidly defined social structures to which Japan attributes its international strength.

The Occupational Group in Context

Among the three social structures that we have examined in detail— the workplace, the school, and the family—we have seen that it is the workplace that most adamantly resists the returnee's reentry. This resistance has little basis in functional concerns—that is, in questions concerning the employee's ability adequately to perform his occupational role. The stigma attached to the returnee in the workplace seems to stem primarily from his breaking of ties—his absence from the group. This absence, coupled with the exposure to alternative work settings, is perceived as threatening to the highly structured and predictable Japanese work setting.

Functional concerns about performance are somewhat more appropriate in the schools, where students may in fact give evidence of lost language ability or erosion of other skills required for successful performance in the examinations. Clearly, efforts are made to get returnee children back on track, but that is only possible if their absence has been short and if they, in essence, renounce any attraction they may have felt for foreign ways. Japanese schools (like all schools) provide children not only with cognitive skills but also with proper socialization. The socialization required for performance in the Japanese occupational structure involves predictability and homogeneity. Behavior that stands out is to be immediately discouraged in returnee children. Even a peanut-butter-and-jelly sandwich is symbolically disruptive.

Mothers work with the educational system to keep children on track. A returnee mother who has perhaps enjoyed increased independence in a foreign country must prove to her community that she will renounce this in Japan in favor of her duties to support those in her family who are engaged in the serious business of school and work. The Japanese mother proves her willingness to resume her role, like the rest of the family, by being ultra-Japanese. She may prove her loyalty in different ways. The woman who abandoned her California halter tops and shorts, another who put a Scandinavian fur coat in storage, and all who recropped their hair and let their perms grow out in the style of the Japanese mother may have neighbors who can wear foreign-style clothing with impunity—but the neighbors' membership was never called into question by a sojourn overseas.

Various kinds of groups do exist in Japan, and various forms of membership. Although one cannot work for two companies, membership in more than one group can coexist if their requirements do not conflict. A housewife can join both a ward action committee and a bridge club. One does not belong, however, to two groups demanding the commitment and loyalty typified by the three primary groups that provide a person with his or her basic identity. Such overlap is scarcely likely since the demands of membership in the groups take so much time.

Groups differ in the amount of time, commitment, and intensity expected of their members. In a work team, rank, function, and other characteristic among members do not carry with them status or any sense of preferential expectation. This is why the president of a Japanese company is often found on the factory floor and vice-ministers work long hours into the night. Similarly, in the traditional family, mothers-in-law wake early to work even harder than their daughters-in-law. For all of them, the time and commitment to the group guarantees their membership in it, and the devotion shown is in itself the substance of their identity within the group. Thus, for the Japanese the completion of tasks does not constitute fulfillment of duty but rather the actvice presence and involvement in the process of fulfilling duty.

Japanese mothers who meet on nice days in a neighborhood playground cannot give long hours to the group formed. In unusual cases the group might become committed to a goal—for instance, a drive to improve play equipment or street lighting in the neighborhood—and hence develop substantial cohesiveness. But mostly the mothers gather for mutual support and advice (exchange) and for the pleasure of meeting each other (relationships). The women educate each other directly (child-rearing information and household hints) and indirectly (observation of each other's dress, disciplinary methods, and the like) and can occasionally watch each other's children. Because their children and households demand their time and primary commitment, such a group cannot be the major source of identity for anyone in it. But it provides enough benefits to ensure that members will appear regularly, and it may even become semiformalized into a locally-known playground-*kai* (group).

A college ski club is an example of the intensity and unifocality of a Japanese group. Designated as a group sharing a specific interest—skiing—the club provides tips on technique, travel, purchase of equipment, and other arrangements directly related to the sport. But most college interest groups seem to have something more diffuse and long-range as a goal. Over the years, they become permanent, cohort-based groups. Relationships within them are often deeper and longer-lasting than other relationships of youth and persist throughout a member's life. Through the group, business deals are made, sons or nephews hired, and daughters married—long after the skiing has ended.

How are these relationships forged? The active core membership of a typical college ski club comprises offspring or connections of the club's alumni—often with little interest in the sport. The group has a seniority system, but hierarchy doesn't have to preclude informality: *sempai* and *kohai* (juniors and seniors) treat each other with greater camaraderie than in official university settings. The new recruits are initiated each year into the rites and relationships of the group, and these typically provide many excuses for parties. Otherwise, exercise sessions, equipment preparation, and trip planning take up many off-season hours. Ideas that seem deliberately to create more interaction are generated; hence, spring, summer, and fall are as activity filled as midwinter. Meeting my college-age research assistant one hot July day, I asked her to join me for a cold drink, but I was told it was her ski club's meeting day and they were off to the seashore. Frequent and regular meetings, whatever the season or activity, forge the relationships that are everyone's real agenda.

In the office work team there are certainly deadlines and periods of time given over entirely to pushing a product out the door. But these do not give the group its identity-conferring characteristic. Instead, individual identity and self-worth are conferred by the constancy and exclusivity of the group's face-to-face relationships. More than other units, this group can demand total time commitment—and absence can mean reintegration problems. The membership of such office groups may change as frequently as every year or two—due to advancements—so intensity and exclusivity may not produce long-term relationships and the achievement of goals; hence, the group's coherence depends on its members' full participation.

In sum, the function of the Japanese group may be to exchange service and information, to tie a member to a network of long-term relationships, to reach a goal or make a product, or to provide a milieu in which cohesion itself, achieved through the constancy of interaction, becomes the purpose of getting together. In Japan, ends and means, product and process, are not clearly differentiated.

Because belonging to the office work group assumes constant attendance and interaction, leaving it presents great risks. Cultural factors—the sense of inside and outside and the maintenance of behavioral, linguistic, and sartorial signals of membership—contribute to the boundary as well but are less important than the heavy time investment demanded by the group.

These facts offer another way to understand why the occupational returnee finds it hard to come back. Not only are the boundaries around the work group most tightly drawn, but the returnee faces a large corporation or government ministry intent on maintaining a domestic focus. As we have seen, the role of international work in

Japan has been set up to protect the mainstream from structural or other "contamination." This has been done, however, without actually creating a class of people who might find satisfying identities as internationals. In other words, the typical returnee has been assigned an often-important task as an individual but has not been assigned to a work team in an organization that can give him a fulfilling identity.

This is an unhappy situation. By being compartmentalized in a zone socially irrelevant to the Japanese group, the international worker protects that group. He maintains the efficiency and "neatness" of a Japanese group by performing in isolation the unpredictable or potentially disruptive acts of international exchange that demand un-Japanese independent initiative and skill specialization. He comes out of his circumstances with only the individual designation of international worker, not the membership in a group he must have to be a well-integrated, normal Japanese.

Brokering and Boundary Defense

We move now from questions of boundary definition to questions of their defense. By what methods are boundaries defended? Why are the criteria of membership so immutable in the face of so much media attention to the problem of the returnee? What motivates—and what is the goal of—the preservation of the status quo?

Generally speaking, occupational boundaries are defended by the use of a specialized and isolated class of international brokers. The isolation and low status of such individuals testify to the perceived threat of boundary crossing within the mainstream of society.

In most societies those who play international roles enjoy high status. Diplomats and international business leaders are often admired and envied for the lives they lead. The jet-setter personifies luxury, while the Peace Corps worker and missionary find purpose and adventure in exotic realms.

In Japan, however, it is contrary to deeply entrenched values to yearn for foreign lands or to explore alternative ways of living. Therefore the foreign encounters required for the conduct of international business must be performed by individuals who are for the most part allowed little responsibility and status. So it is that those who make the real decisions about how to conduct Japan's relationships with the rest of the world are shielded from direct contact with foreigners by these nearly pariah-like brokers. These people provide a protective barrier between high status and international contact.

Here is an example of the difficult role of the broker, though in this instance an American plays the role:

A Japanese company president pays a visit to an American company president at the American's office. They talk through an American interpreter, who works for the American company but is well acquainted with Japanese business customs. The Japanese is in his late sixties; the American, in his early fifties. The Japanese has come to pay his respects in a friendly but formal way to a man whom he sees as representing an equivalent of his (very prestigious) firm, though he is surprised at the youth of a man in a position that is not attained in the Japanese seniority system until later in life. Through the interpreter, the Japanese expresses his pleasure at their meeting and his wishes for the success of future meetings. The American president takes these expressions literally and says, "Well, why don't we get down to business now?" The Japanese repeats his hope that *in the future* they may enter into a profitable joint venture.

The American president thinks the Japanese has cold feet. In an aside, the interpreter tells him that Japanese business is conducted in gradual stages but assures him that there is basic good feeling and eventually matters will be settled to the mutual satisfaction of both. The American becomes annoyed, and says, "I'm not here to talk about culture. This is business!" The interpreter feels he must mediate the outburst and awkwardly covers for the American by saying to the Japanese, "Mr. X. presents his compliments to your wife and hopes he can meet with you in Tokyo."

Here the interpreter is not simply a translator but a "culture broker"[8]—a one-man buffer zone between different systems. He is culturally sensitive to both, but in the interests of his own company and job security, he must "lie for the boss"—and yet he feels he must also make the visit acceptable for the Japanese. The broker will have to coach his boss for later encounters, but if a deal does not materialize, the American boss will think that the broker failed to do his work.

Although all three are part of this international episode, the broker's role is specifically international. If a deal goes through, the go-between will be regarded as successful and valued by his American boss. But the Japanese executive sees the translator's work as merely linguistic and mechanical. If business develops, the Japanese will give no credit to the culture broker, who is only a functionary and in no way a creator.

This separation of high status from international contact perplexes many American businessmen, even though they are told that their Japanese counterparts in business negotiations are not empowered or elite brokers. As one writer put it, "They are [international] Japanese . . . a species of clerk designed to keep foreigners happy."[9] The reality may frustrate and confuse Americans, who may then question Japanese sincerity as well as the merit and finality of the negotiations.

Another complementary role of the broker is to furnish a protective barrier of formality. Diplomats who work directly with the Japanese are likely to understand and respect Japanese distancing through formality, unlike the American company president who expected to "get down to business." The product of most diplomatic exchanges is, in any case, more given over to rapport than to orders and contracts.

Resistance at the Boundary of the Uchi

Given the nature of Japanese membership, especially occupational membership, it is not hard to understand why absentee employees suffer from a sense of not belonging. Yet the severity of the handicaps resulting from their absence and the resistance they face to their reintegration raises questions about the operation of the conservative forces that maintain the status quo. Why are the changes that might result from exposure to foreign ways so threatening What is at stake?

Generally speaking, what is being defended is the Japanese uchi, the preservation of a homogeneous island identity. That special, exclusive, and embattled sense of being Japanese and the preservation of a relatively smoothly functioning and complex social structure supports successful competition in the international arena. The two realities are paradoxical but not at all contradictory: The first is in the service of the second. Japan is in fact a small island nation that takes pride in its heritage and uniqueness. Japan's history is one of relative isolation, and even now it tries to draw strength from within, eschewing cultural and political dependence on larger states even as its resource dependence increases. Japan's sources of strength over the centuries have varied, but after World War II, its basic source of international strength has of course been economic, and that is something to be fiercely defended.

In other arenas of international competition, a sense of pride may mask an uncomfortable reality, as in the response to Japan's poor showing in the 1976 Winter Olympics in Innsbruck. A newspaper article in Japan explained their failure, saying, "They didn't do well at Innsbruck, since it is hard competing overseas with foreigners, but back in Japan they are more comfortable and confident and they show their true ability."

Within Japan, we find a society whose social structures—educational, familial, and occupational—operate smoothly in a complementary fashion to produce a highly trained and devoted work force. Disruption in any one of these spheres may upset the whole and thereby jeopardize national economic strength. For example, women cannot be both ideal mothers and ideal employees. They cannot both work late at the office and wait on the every need of their student-children. Both roles are seen as too demanding to be done well simultaneously. While in American society the juggling of many roles may indeed present problems, each individual chooses a different set of compromises, utilizing baby-sitters, working part-time, negotiating with her spouse. The Japanese workplace offers no role of importance to a part-time worker, and a part-time Japanese mother cannot perform adequately, as she is not fully available for the support of her child's education—an education that is of great importance to occupational success.

Similarly, exposure to new working styles invites judgments concerning the complex but predictable functioning of the office team. Returnees often find that they have become unaccustomed to the rules of the Japanese office. They find bothersome and somewhat incomprehensible the time-consuming, interdependent, and diffuse relationships in the organization. Yet, if the returnee is to be accepted, he must relearn the rules and attempt to reweave the web of connection.

Exposure to alternative lifestyles—that is, more options in women's lives, more questioning of authority, more competitive and innovative individual action at the office—threatens the standardization of the social system, and thus the economic strength on which Japan depends for its sense of security and independence.

The standardization of life—what I earlier called "the yappari factor"—is not only an efficient means of promoting economic success. It is also a cultural tradition. The Japanese sought safety in similarity long before World War II or the oil crisis of 1973. Japan finds its sense of identity not in political principles and plurality (like the United States) and not in a shared religious tradition (like Iran) but in a sense of its uniqueness as a people. To outsiders it has projected that uniqueness. Within its borders individuals must embody that uniform uniqueness in all details if they are to belong. Once again, we find a paradox as the outside meets the inside: An ideal of conformity shapes the lives of people who take pride in their national uniqueness.

Such deeply entrenched social conformity as we find in one Japanese group is not simply a process; it is an end in itself. One cosmopolitan banker I interviewed said, "The Japanese are as homogeneous as a plain white silk fabric. We all try to stay that way, or if we aren't, to become that way."

Japanese social structures define relationships and lines of loyalty with little ambiguity. While one may be a member of a work team, a family, and a ski club, there is little room for conflicting loyalties because the groups have clearly ordered relative priorities. While Americans may agonize over setting priorities in their personal lives, the Japanese suffer relatively little from such conflicts (unless, of course, faced with international assignments).

If lines of loyalty are clear, we can see why international work is stigmatized as disloyal. In Japan competing sets of loyalties are studiously avoided. Either one is or one isn't a loyal office team member. If a worker isn't at the office, defining his membership through active presence, he must be elsewhere, a member of some other group. So he must have shifted his primary alliegance elsewhere, have found a new locus of identity outside the old group. Hence, multiple memberships are seen as suspect and are discouraged. A Japanese college student, for example, usually gives himself over to one activity, and finds the long lists of club affiliations in an American college yearbook puzzling.

What a Japanese misses by diversifying his loyalties or by his absence from the source of primary identity may be understood by reference to an American high school football team. Missing four days of practice puts a team member at a serious disadvantage, and missing practice becomes a recurrent theme of nightmares among players. That pit-of-the-stomach feeling of panic and isolation approximates the tenor of feeling for the Japanese international, and it might be said that, in this regard, belonging to a Japanese group is like belonging to an American football team.

Taboos on travel exist elsewhere in the world, but they are differently observed and buffered. India is a society with a tightly organized social structure and a religious taboo against travel, but it offers a culturally acceptable route for circumventing problems. Brahmin elites are expected to observe cultural rules more stringently than persons of lower caste. But because of economic and political advantages, some members of this caste are more apt to transgress them by "crossing the black waters" or by eating forbidden meat with foreign friends and to become impure. Yet, thanks to the existence of "repurification" rites, Brahmins need not become permanently stigmatized but are readmitted to full membership after a simple ritual.[10] Outsider status only develops when the individual chooses not to cleanse away his or her contact with the outside.

While Indian elites come from a highly organized traditional society, a Hindu international can go home much more readily than a Japanese international, to whom no redemptive ritual is available. I would suggest that the difference stems from the fact that Indian communities do not perceive themselves as at all homogeneous. Instead, they possess a high degree of internal differentiation by race, religion, caste, and occupation. Because in India there is an expectation that in everyday life many structural boundaries will be crossed and recrossed, the crossings are marked with suitable rituals and customs to accommodate potential pollution, given a tightly organized and mutually dependent social diversity.

It may be that the ideal of homogeneity in Japan is actually promoted by the stigmatization attached to foreign contact. The returnee symbolizes transgression and thereby represents a sort of photographic negative of the Japanese ideal.[11] This is to say that Japanese cultural values may be perpetuated and enforced less by people who succeed, and more by people who *fail* to embody the norm. In other words, negative models preserve homogeneity more than idealized persons or heroic figures. The negative example marks the boundary between the acceptable and the inappropriate, as well as a cautionary reminder of the price one may pay. The stigmatizing of the returnee who has gone "beyond the pale" heightens the negative role that he plays, and counteracts whatever attractive aspects of international contact may surface.

An International Future? How Far Can the Uchi Be Stretched?

The mood and realities confronting at least some returning families has begun to change. Since 1985 universities have offered special entrance examinations to returning students, and it is reported that prestigious ministries, such as MITI, now reserve some jobs specifically for returnee applicants. This is concrete evidence that attention is being paid to the problems returnees have in gaining admission to mainstream education and careers and, perhaps, to the contributions they might be able to make as students and employees. The word *eigoya*, a derogatory term meaning "seller of English," is less frequently used, and speakers of English are receiving higher status, if still tied to their linguistic function. Very recent returnees (1985–87) report that those who have completed high school overseas now have fewer problems than before because of special entrance exams into colleges that have new quotas for returnees. But younger children remain at risk and continue to have both personal and institutional adjustment problems. It appears that the occupational system, and colleges linked to it, is less conservative than the educational system, which has not responded to the threat posed to returnee children's life chances. However, it remains to be seen if the returnees finding work and study in domestic institutions are to be streamed as internationals or to be hired and trained as normal Japanese. Or it may be in the long run that the occupational and educational worlds will themselves internationalize, ridding themselves of the need to stigmatize and compartmentalize.

Japan's international paradox has now become an international problem. The tension that exists between Japan and the rest of the world is at a postwar high. The issues of trade imbalance are complex, and other players, especially the United States, bring their own worries, weaknesses, and stereotypes to bear on the situation. It is clear, however, that the Japanese come into the international arena favoring a cultural Achilles heel, which compounds many problems in trade and diplomatic exchange. Documented here is Japan's international handicap made concrete by the lives of the ordinary people who have borne the brunt of both domestic and international pressures.

Where will the Hayashis, Kajimas, and Fujimuras find themselves in the next twenty years? The international teenager of today may become the ordinary "salary men" of tomorrow or may still be asking that the rhetorical emphasis on kokusaika, (internationalization) be turned into realities they can live by. In any case the children may not follow in the paths of the parents. Except for those who really cannot reenter a normal Japanese school, or who have attended high school overseas and thus have missed the terrifying but formative experience that shapes their peers' lives, a meritocratic model still prevails, and a child may pass into the domestic mainstream by passing the right tests. The important question is, What is tested and selected by the meritocratic system and what excluded? Current discussions in educational reform do involve kokusaika. The hope is to broaden the international perspective of textbooks and classrooms in Japan, particularly by introducing better foreign language instruction. Certainly the Japanese curriculum could be internationalized. But one might wonder if what is taught—assuming reform is thoroughly implemented— will be valued and perpetuated in universities and in the workplace. For what counts ultimately is the set of values embodied in the policies and practices of the workplace. Like the schools that teach what is testable in the exams, these policies and priorities will determine a child's future and the future of internationalization in Japan. But even more important than the content of the curriculum or the values of the workplace is the structure of the educational system and the workplace—the ways in which the institutions guide the path of the individual: The uchi may persist even as the style and skills of individuals become international.

What we are really talking about, then, is not personal experiences, interpretations, and strategies, not school curricula or personnel management policy. Japan remains a macro-uchi, and given the corporate entities within it that reproduce the identity-conferring and loyalty-demanding aspects of the traditional household—a flexible approach to the outside world becomes a very difficult enterprise.

Some change is occurring—more midcareer job changes, more interest in concrete skills over generalist abilities, and a stated interest in diversifying educational tracks. But as long as the relationships and identities that give meaning to life are governed by specific rules and expectations, by a need for predictability and consensus rather than more "portable," flexible, and abstract criteria, people who do not meet the standards will continue to be seen as different whatever anybody's intentions.

International Choices in an Uchi Society

Today the decision to become an international person is a decision to be functional but suspect. Parents cannot promise their children a normal Japanese life if they opt for nonmainstream, international schooling, and few would deliberately assume that risk. But more parents are choosing to keep their children with them overseas through high school now, which has forced the introduction of special exams for those who have had secondary education abroad. Meanwhile, more companies are sending more workers overseas. And while the employees may suffer the effects of compartmentalization on their return to Japan, their very numbers will clearly achieve some sort of critical mass. The sidetrack may have to be acknowledged as an alternative main track—something hard for traditional managers and companies to envision and accept today.

It is not clear that the efforts and institutional accommodations currently being made for returnees to readjust and reassimilate are effective. Are parents using special classes actually giving their children benefits or further marking them as different? Are those returnees who seek to become 100 percent again by anxious strategems actually succeeding and, if so, what have they gained? It will take more time and more data before answers can be given to these and other questions raised in my study. If what we see are simply the last throes of a Japanese cultural battle to remain pure in the face of the international demands of the modern world, we should before long see change in the returnees' lives and in the organizations to which they return. But it is still an important moment, and to understand the realities of Japan's third foray into the world is to understand the force and durability of the institutions and culture that have preserved the uchi and its members thus far.

The Japanese overseas employee is caught between his nation's need of international brokers and the need of his uchi for protection from change. He exists in a cultural no-man's-land. He is a functional deviant, a ferryboatman, rowing the stuff of international exchange back and forth across otherwise uncrossable waters. The stigma attached to his role is explained not by any one social, cultural, or economic factor but by a cluster of such factors: He is regarded as potentially disruptive of the efficient, standardized and loyal work force to which Japan attributes its world success; his absence suspends his relationship-based membership; given unifocal loyalty, he is assumed to be disloyal; and given national homogeneity he must learn the ways of diverse cultures. While essential to Japan's prosperity, the returnee must remain a stigmatized deviant—one who shoulders the burden of Japan's paradoxical identity as an international and yet uniquely isolated nation.

The overseas Japanese is perhaps an unwitting existential hero.

Appendix 1

The Sample and Interviews

To carry out my study, fifty families living in or near Tokyo were interviewed intensively. The family sample was collected through prior connections with persons in businesses and government agencies who had themselves been overseas. Collecting a sample of persons who would cooperate freely with the researcher was greatly facilitated by contacts furnished by friends and associates. A useful random sample of returnees would have been very difficult to obtain in a society where prior contact or the services of a go-between are crucial to the success of any relationship.

My initial contacts were with elite persons in terms of occupation and rank within their company, ministry, or university. I feared that because of the usual homogeneity of associations this would weight my later connections. However, I found that by the third or fourth remove from the initial contacts, the informants were from many different educational, social, and occupational backgrounds. It appears that as returnees begin to associate less on the basis of long-standing personal connections and more as fellow returnees or as a result of shared experiences overseas, this new interest grouping produces a wider range of contacts.

More than 80 percent of all returnees live in the Tokyo area, the site of government ministries and the home offices of companies that send the largest numbers of employees overseas. Tokyo is the locus of the most prestigious domestic work as well, and those with high aspirations will attempt to be posted there. Although they may have little control over their postings, returnees who aim at a mainstream domestic job will try to work in the Tokyo home office. However, being in

Tokyo does not guarantee a prestigious career for a returnee: Many are sidetracked in international sections in the home office, while many domestic employees are sent to branch offices in the hinterlands before returning to top management track positions in Tokyo.

First Sample: School, Work, and Home

Careers and Ages

The sample includes bureaucrats and businessmen working for large companies, banks, and government ministries and teachers in universities. The age range of the sample is from the late twenties to the early forties, with a few persons near retirement (fifty-five to fifty-seven in most companies). Their families are young: Fathers are in their late thirties or early forties, and mothers in the mid- to late thirties. Generally speaking, most families who are sent overseas fall in this age group. It is the policy of most personnel departments to send younger employees whose careers may be less threatened or families whose children are young and thus less vulnerable to dislocation in the educational system. It is commonly considered dangerous to one's progress to travel at a level above subsection chief, a stage reached by the early forties. Overseas postings in this sample thus occurred in the first eight to twelve years of the informant's employment. I interviewed families with children who were junior-high-school age or younger when they were overseas, since I intended to concentrate on the crisis felt in the public educational system through junior high school. The sample includes both families whose children attend the special readjustment schools and families who placed their children directly in ordinary schools.

Length and Place of Sojourn

The length of overseas stay in the group ranges from 2 to 14 years, with the mean at 5.4 years. Businessmen were customarily given posts overseas of about 5 years, while shorter postings were typical of government bureaucrats and university teachers. In general, the smaller the firm, the longer the sojourn, since it is more economical to keep a few families overseas for longer periods than it is to cycle short postings. Recently, however, the sojourns of employees of government ministries and large companies also are lengthening.

It was posited that the location of the overseas sojourn might determine the families' readjustment to Japan. To test this a geographical distribution of overseas posts was included. In general, informants said that return from a developing-country posting is more difficult than that from an advanced nation, but several variables complicated the situation. For example, because local schools are considered inappropriate, Japanese children in developing countries usually had access to full-time overseas Japanese school established by the Ministry of Education, giving them better academic preparation for the return to Japanese schools than that received by children who attended local schools in advanced countries.

Second Sample: The Organization

While much information on the return to a Japanese workplace was gathered in the family interviews, a second sample was collected to gain a more complete picture of the strategies of employing organizations dealing with the "return crisis." This sample consisted of fifty employees, administrators, executives, and personnel managers in the same trading companies, banks, manufacturers, and government agencies that employed the fathers in the family sample. The age and overseas sojourn pattern of,the employees was virtually the same as that of the first sample. General patterns of recruitment and deployment of personnel were traced for each organization, and a complex picture of the treatment and role of the international returnee in his company emerged.

The Interviews

In most cases, interviews were conducted with women at home, men at work, and children at home after school. A few evening and weekend interviews included all family members. Spouses interviewed separately often gave different responses, but in the cases where I interviewed husband and wife together, the wife deferred to the husband. By contrast, children seemed as open and frank in the presence of a parent as they were when alone with the interviewer. Children were always ready to talk about real or imagined injustices and prejudices. They would tell me such things as, "Germans always made me feel more Japanese than I feel here," or, "Since I returned from Thailand, my classmates call me *dojin* [peasant]; do you think my skin really is darker?" Statements like these and the frequent remark that returnees were teasingly called gaijin were corroborated by teachers who said such taunts were often heard at school.

Interviews with housewives were held in their homes, except for those with three women who asked me to meet them together at their husbands' company club in downtown Tokyo. Home interviews gave me a chance to assess life-style and to ask specific questions about accommodation to Japanese living conditions; in many cases, I could also see how much of their overseas life they had brought back in the form of household goods and art objects.

If members of the extended family, such as a mother-in-law, lived in the household, this provided opportunities for questions about relations with family members who had not lived overseas. While there was often some hesitation in discussing these matters (in several cases, the mother-in-law even presided over the interview), women usually responded frankly. They relaxed more in follow-up interviews, and so I attempted to arrange a second meeting in each case. Since the child's educational future is explicitly the mother's responsibility, and since the greatest hardship for the family overseas is the loss of a Japanese education for its children, the problem of the long-term effects of the sojourn weighed heavily on the mothers.

I interviewed the fathers in coffeehouses and bars or in private conference rooms at their offices. They were more relaxed and optimistic in their assessment of the effects of the overseas experience on their families than were their wives but more anxious about their own prospects. As one woman said when I mentioned that her husband had not seemed worried about the children, "Yes, that's my husband's point of view, but he doesn't have to arrange for our child's after-school classes or talk to his teachers when he has trouble at school."

All persons in the sample spoke some English, and several who had been posted in Europe or other non-English-speaking areas spoke other languages as well. The informants' ease in speaking foreign languages was notable, although several said that they tried to speak Japanese as much as possible. Most interviews were conducted in Japanese.

The lengths of the interviews varied considerably. The home interviews were more leisurely and ranged from two to four hours. The workplace interviews were usually about two hours long, but some were two separate one-hour sessions sometimes held on the same day, depending on the pressures of work. In some cases meetings were shortened by the informants' stated concern that a long conference with a foreigner would be deleterious to their nurtured image of a mainstream, domestic-based employee. In a very few cases when a meeting had to be cut short, informants responded later in writing, but the written questionnaire response was invariably thinner than the conversations.

Other Interviews and Resources

The study included several group interviews. In each school I visited, I conducted informal group discussions among returned students in which we discussed academic and personal readjustment to Japan. I arranged meetings with a group of returnee students who were themselves studying the problem of intercultural communication at several universities in Tokyo. Four of these students were writing undergraduate or master's theses on the problems of children who return to Japan from overseas. I also participated in informal group meetings with housewives who had recently returned, in which we discussed readjustment schools and classes and their own experiences of reentry in Japan. I was also invited to sit in during teachers' evaluation discussions of returned children, and to teach and interview at one of the schools for returnees.

Group discussions in Japan have their own flavor, and I hesitate to take the material gained in these at face value. Generally, however, my presence seems to have catalyzed rather than prevented discussion. In some cases I felt that the objectivity and "outsider" aspects of my role helped people express themselves freely. The fact that these groups were ad hoc groups brought together for my research meant that the members—while somewhat awkward in their dealings with each other—did not have to obey the rules of a previously established relationship with all its time- and content-consuming etiquette. Nor did they show restraint in expressing opinions and disagreeing with each other. Besides, the very nature of the material, involving a relatively new awareness of a boundary, meant that there were few established ideas people would feel tied to, and they could express themselves easily in terms of their own experiences. Indeed, it seems as though some were relieved to have an opportunity for this expression. (I also saw this need in the fact that once my project became known, I had absolutely no difficulty in arranging meetings and in interviewing people—in fact, I often received calls from people I didn't know, asking me to interview them. Another researcher in Japan found that her project, interviewing grandmothers, met with the same kind of response: These people seem to lack a forum for discussion and welcome opportunities such as those we presented.)

Although the presence of a foreigner may have interfered, it seems that my being an obvious outsider may have helped more than it hindered. First of all, as many interviewers have noticed, people will often be more open with an outsider than with an insider. Particularly in Japan, where these categories have great weight, an outsider is at a paradoxical advantage. I was explicitly told several times that I was getting information the informant would not have given to a Japanese. Second, where my role as a foreigner presented problems, it provoked a response that itself reflected the issues under investigation, as in the case cited in chapter 5, when my unexpected appearance at an informant's office led to an almost melodramatic attempt to "cover" the incident.

Another interview effect was noted. As an American, the interviewer was sometimes seen as the representative of a "superior" culture. This sometimes led to humble or disparaging remarks about Japanese society in comparisons of educational or occupational systems but also gave especially disaffected returnees a chance to express strong feelings about the seniority system or the "closed," vertical society of Japan and gave others a chance to compare Japanese society favorably to foreign societies. Although it was sometimes difficult to tell whether a negative remark about Japan represented a returnee's disaffection or "courtesy to a foreigner," in context the remarks did correlate with the individual's relative alienation or reassimilation.

Data on overseas and returnee education, the growing literature in the field, and interviews with overseas and returnee Japanese were updated in 1984 and 1985 from the original research conducted in 1975–76.

Appendix 2

Cities and Wards Receiving Returnee Children

Beside the private and specially subsidized "receiving schools," there are thirteen "receiving cities and wards," as follows:

City/Ward	Number of Elementary Schools	Number of Middle Schools
Omiya City, Saitama Prefecture	35	20
Funabashi City, Chiba	53	28
Chiyoda Ward, Tokyo	14	5
Meguro Ward, Tokyo	22	12
Setagaya Ward, Tokyo	64	32
Suginami Ward, Tokyo	43	23
Nerima Ward, Tokyo	62	30
Miyamae, Aso Ward, Kawasaki	24	15
Totsuka Ward, Yokohama	52	22
Chikusa, Meito Ward, Nagoya	32	17
Toyonaka City, Osaka	40	19
Kobe City, Hyogo Prefecture	164	74
Nishinomiya City, Hyogo Prefecture	39	17

These jurisdictions provide support for students in ward and city schools through classes and programs. It should be noted that the Kobe area has a large number of such schools and has traditionally been an "international" site for foreign business and contact.

Appendix 3

Characteristics and Strategies of the Sample

Characteristics

Occupational Sample

(N = 68)
49 male
19 female

Average Age on Return to Japan

40.1 years

Educational Background

Tokyo, Kyoto universities	31 (46%)
Other Japanese universities	30 (44%)
Foreign universities	7 (10%)

Type of Occupation

Government	
Ministry of Finance	5
Ministry of Foreign Affairs	5

Ministry of Eduction	3
Ministry of Justice	1
Subtotal	14
Trading Companies	10
Other Domestic	
Banking	5
Industry	4
Industrial research	4
Medicine	1
International or foreign firms	9
Academic	14
Media	7
Subtotal:	44
Total:	68

Categories of Work

These groupings were suggested by informants, personnel officers, executives, and experts in Japanese business. While the character of the organization affects the employee's readjustment to Japan after overseas sojourns, his or her personal strategy also affects his or her ultimate characterization as "domestic" or "international."

Domestic		International	
Ministries of Finance, Education, and Justice	9	Ministry of Affairs, trading companies	15
Banking, industry, medicine, academic, research	28	International firms, foreign companies, media	16
Total	37	Total	31

Overseas Postings (Most Recent)

United States	55
Europe and Australia	9
Latin America, Africa, and Southeast Asia	4
Average Length of Last Overseas Post	2.75 years

Average Length of Sojourns Overseas

Domestic		International	
Type of Firm	Years	Type of Firm	Years
Finance Ministry	3	Ministry of Foreign Affairs	3
Ministry of Education	2.5	Trading Companies	3.5
Ministry of Justice	1.0	International Business	2.5
Banking	3	Foreign Companies	4
Industry	5	Media	1.5
Medicine	1.5	Average	2.9
Academic	1.5		
Average	2.5		

Taking each of the variables into consideration, we can judge the effect of personal and institutional conditions on the readjustment of returnees and attempt to correlate personal strategies with type of occupation.

Age and Status

An important factor affecting strategies of return and employees' anxieties is relative age and status within the firm. The average returnee in the sample has been in his company for about fifteen years and has children approaching middle school age (about twelve–fourteen years). After this stage in his work life, the employee can find fewer overseas posts of a status appropriate to a rising career, and at home as well the career posts shrink in number. His children are at a similar stage, where competition for places in high-prestige middle and high schools is great. The father has little control over his own precarious position and focuses on the children's problem. One might surmise that parental anxiety over children in the educational system is at least in part a projection of a sense of crisis in the father's career.

Educational Background

Those who did not attend the most elite and prestigious universities said that those who had would have little trouble assimilating to Japan and that a major factor in their own troubles was poor educational credentials. However, those who had gone to Tokyo and Kyoto universities, the leading national universities, did not agree and said that they had encountered special problems in spite of their elite education. Their own more mainstream and domestic background, they averred, meant that their differentness was more striking. In this case, they felt that elite did not mean privileged but that their credentials only gave them initial access to mainstream advancement tracts. Those who had gone to foreign universities had given up a normal Japanese life and sought or accepted the "international" designation.

Type of Occupation and Categories of Work

The organization employing the largest number of members of the sample is the Japanese government. Within this group, however, there was a wide range of types of employment, from career posts to liaison and staff. Trading-company jobs accounted for the next largest group, whose experiences were more homogeneous. Banking and other domestic firms accounted for most of the remainder, which included several in independent research institutes and in academic professions. Finally, nine were in foreign or international work.

Overseas Postings and Length of Stay

These groupings (United States, Europe and Australia, Latin America, Africa, Southeast Asia) correspond to those used by personnel divisions in making cycled assignments: The first two are considered on the whole to be good posts, the last group to be hardship posts. While some of the sample had had previous posts in the Middle East, none had more recent ones there. Middle Eastern (OPEC) posts are now moving into the Europe and Australia category due to the importance to Japan of energy resources. Nine of those whose last posting was the United States had previously been sent to countries in the third category. Information on the experiences of overseas employees in these locations was drawn from interviews with all persons in the occupational and family samples who had at any time resided in a developing nation.

Posts are valued differently by different occupations: Paris is important for international organizations: Geneva, Frankfurt, or London for banking; Washington and New York for diplomacy and business; and

Houston and Los Angeles for industry. The most prestigious posts seem to be those that are in "high-ranked" countries (as above) and that involve constant communication with the home office. Being in close touch with Japan and maintaining the communication that will determine their future posts makes these assignments attractive to many. Communication seems to be even more important than the relative prestige of the posting, though of course the "best" places also have the best contact with Japan, either through good communications networks or through large concentrations of Japanese overseas offices and plants.

Personnel managers of large companies usually try to alternate employees' assignments between posts in developing and advanced nations and try to bring them home between overseas postings. But certain assignments are said to be clear indications that one has long been pushed off the tract (sent to "Siberia"), and too long a posting in an insignificant office will be dangerous to one's career. Several who reported having been sent to remote places for long periods (to Alaska for six years, for example) used the phrase *shima nagashi*, meaning "banishment," as of a criminal, "to an island exile," to describe their assignments.

The length of stay overseas is thought to be crucial to the success or failure of full readjustment in Japan. The longest sojourns tend to be those in industry, foreign business, and trading companies. The shortest are those of "independent" travelers in medicine, academic life, and the media—or those on training or research leaves to foreign universities from such government ministries, as the Ministry of Justice. Although informants say that length of post abroad is crucial, I found that actual overseas stays are roughly similar and that time overseas actually becomes a problem only when an employee is given several different consecutive overseas postings or when for unusual reasons his stay is extended. In the opinion of most, five years is the limit. Because their cases seemed significantly different for reasons other than their longer postings, I chose not to include in the sample four informants whose overseas sojourns exceeded ten years.

Appendix 4

International Work in Various Organizations

Academic, banking, and Foreign Ministry careers are described in the text. Work in another government bureaucracy, typified by the Finance Ministry, and work in trading companies, international or foreign organizations, and the media were also represented in the sample and are described below.

Government Bureaucracy

Ministries whose work is primarily domestic can be distinguished from those whose work involves much international contact. However, even those with many overseas posts can be characterized as domestic in employment structure, criteria for personnel advancement, and in the values that shape the experience of overseas employees. In considering the work of these ministries I will consider persons on the so-called elite career track (*kyariaa gumi*), because it is they who experience the most tension and displacement as a result of their international work. The Finance Ministry's recruitment, training, and advancement patterns are typical of those of domestic government agencies.

Job placement within the ministry is determined by successful performance on one of three entrance examinations. Career officers have passed examinations in categories 1 (*jokyū*) and 2 (*chukyū*). Staff have passed category 3 (*shokyū*) examinations. Those who are admitted under the first examination are the elite career-path entrants. The word *career* here, as elsewhere, describes those who climb the fastest promotion ladder leading to vice-ministerial or other top-level posts. These people are from top universities, most often from Tokyo University's law department, and have often taken the examination after a fifth year of training.

Finance Ministry

In the Finance Ministry, career bureaucrats tend to be products of the Tokyo University law department. This is a self-perpetuating connection, in that professors or "old boys" help later graduates to enter. But connections alone are not enough; the top-level entrance examinations are difficult and guarantee that entrants are able and hardworking. The work in the ministry is chiefly domestic and yet, like much of Japanese business, highly dependent on the external world. In recent years, as a consequence, half of every entering group was assigned to an overseas post within their first eight to ten years within the ministry.

Recently overseas posts have become so common that it is possible under the right conditions for an elite-track employee to remain on his career path even after an overseas sojourn. Previously such a post would have marked him as a specialist. However, even now avoiding this appellation requires much attention to the timing and conditions of the overseas stay.

As in other domestic ministries, there are two streams in the Finance Ministry: the domestic and the international. Bureaucrats themselves sometimes claim membership in the *kokunaiha* or *kokusaiha* (domestic or international factions). The structure of work and relationships in the first is characterized by traditional networks and negotiations and by a sense of being one family. This attitude balances or softens the other major characteristics of the group—ambition and personal interest in the dynamics of power. Among those in the international stream, there is a feeling that they have been typecast by their overseas experience, which they tend to blame for pushing them off-track. While increasing numbers of even top-level or elite employees have overseas sojourns at some point in their careers, international typing happens only to those who are frequently reassigned overseas or who develop strong language skills.

Education and training often influence one's future status in the ministry. Every year, twenty to twenty-five new workers are recruited to the ministry through the career-level examination. They work for the Ministry in home office posts for two years. Four or five of them are then chosen for training in foreign universities (two or three of these are sent to universities in the United States). At the same time, others are sent for training in the Foreign Ministry Training Institute as preparation for work as attachés to Japanese embassies and consulates. This training lasts five months and consists chiefly of language study. The graduates of this program are then lent to the Foreign Ministry as economic advisers for the term of their overseas postings (usually three to four years in an advanced nation, two to three years in a developing nation). There are, altogether, sixty ministry employees overseas at any time, thirty-five of whom are temporarily attached to the Foreign Ministry. The remainder are members of special task forces or on special missions.

Finance Ministry bureaucrats are especially sensitive to the requirements of the career path, and those interviewed were consistent in their descriptions of the elite path. It is possible, they said, to be both elite and international, but only if one follows certain guidelines. In an embassy post, for instance, it is important to do home-based work that focuses on Japanese domestic issues. In Japan one should do domestic work but serve as an occasional emissary to international conferences. From the Finance Ministry, elite internationals are often sent for short assignments to the International Monetary Fund, the World Bank, or the Asian Development Bank.

Informants said any overseas posting should occur early in one's career, before the periods of "narrowing the pyramid" in which one's advancement depends on constant attention to the personal networks of the organization. By the age of forty, one's foreign experiences should be over: The late thirties are testing years, and it is felt that one should be in the home office to ensure advancement. Of course, there is little room for direct negotiation over a career, and most employees simply observe their own path as they evolve. But careers can be affected by relationships with superiors. Whether or not a bureau chief is willing to recommend a worker to a more prestigious bureau depends on his relationship with that worker. The recent entrant and the overseas worker have the least-developed relationships and are naturally more vulnerable in the job reshuffle, which may happen as often as every two years.

The safe or preferred paths are well known, and most jobs can be tagged as creditable or damaging. Employees say that the best jobs in the Finance Ministry are the "hard" domestic ones in the Budget and Tax divisions, and the worst are the "soft" positions in international monetary fields. An elite career path is said to follow a pattern like this:

Years after Entry	Post
1–3	Domestic, home-office training
4–6	District office in Japan
7–9	Home office, different bureau
10	Mainstream, home office—tax or budget

If this path were to include an overseas sojourn, it would begin with a training period in the home office. Then the recruit would be sent for language and orientation to the Foreign Ministry Training Institute and overseas as an attaché to the Japanese embassy in Paris, Bonn, Washington, or (more recently) Kuwait or Saudi Arabia. On return the employee would serve as a local tax commissioner in a district office in a place such as Sendai or Fukuoka—far from Tokyo but not insignificant. The next post would take him back to Tokyo for a mainstream job in the budget office, where he would be part of the brain trust of a high official.

The above description fits a few very elite returnees. Most returnees are subjected to some sort of sidetracking or international compartmentalization. One kind of sidetracking is temporary assignment to a floating, taskless job. When a person returns from overseas, he often first enters a so-called "waiting post," of which there are many at many levels. These posts have no specific tasks attached to them but carry a full salary and assignment to a desk. One kind of waiting post, which is intended to help the returnee relearn the skills of the home office, is in the International Bureau. However, according to many, they can easily be assigned there permanently if they have been too internationalized by their overseas sojourn. While most of these permanently international employees are nonelites to begin with, some career-track returnees find themselves asked to perform the functions of the benriya (utility men) or eigoya (English peddlers) who translate, interpret, and serve as guides for foreign visitors—jobs usually given to non-career-track international specialists. These returnees said their tasks center on protocol and on petty details of conferences and meetings—preparing the way for others more generalist and elite. These people compare themselves to the *kurokata,* the stage-hands dressed in black who serve to prepare the scenes and arrange the costumes of the main actors in Japanese traditional theater. One sees the figures, of course, but after a while one doesn't "see" them, paying attention only to the events they are arranging.

The International Bureau is on a separate line, which does not lead to top leadership positions. However, there are certain advantages to being in this bureau. Although an International Bureau employee cannot aspire to the vice-ministership (the position of greatest actual power), he does have a greater chance of being head of his bureau, whereas those in domestic bureaus, because of their large numbers, must compete energetically for advancement.

In the Ministry of Finance, as in most Japanese business and government posts, personnel managers attempt to cycle overseas posts. Personnel policy emphasizes equal sharing of the burden of increased international work, and some managers say that spreading the duty around will eventually make the work less stigmatizing. From the point of view of the employees, however, whether they are explicitly sidetracked in the International Bureau or not, they face problems of integration in the ministry. An employee who anticipates these problems before departure will establish a friend in the office as a "career caretaker" who will look out for his interests. This person must be selected carefully, however, for cases were reported of caretakers who took advantage of their friends and leapfrogged over them—a rare and perfidious act.

In sum, the Ministry of Finance continues to have a strong domestic orientation and a restricted elite career track. It compartmentalizes returnees in the International Bureau, isolating them by the specialization of their international tasks and insulating the home office from their differentness and unpredictability. If, however, an employee has been abroad at the right time (early), briefly, and in the right places (advanced countries) doing nonspecialist work, his experience can be an advantage to him. The number of these "properly" situated returnees is not great, and the experience of reentry into the ministry remains problem filled.

Trading Companies

Trading companies, the large and complex links between Japanese business and world markets and resources, are interesting to any analysis of internationalization and its costs and benefits. These companies are obviously international: they do most of the international business of buying and selling raw materials, selling finished goods, and negotiating Japanese overseas manufacturing and industrial development, although an increasing share of their business is as a third party—buying and selling as go-betweens for two other nations. Since the volume of international business conducted by these companies is so great, it might be thought that the large numbers of employees involved in such work would internationalize the company's structure and work style. And yet, perhaps *because* of the overtly international character of the work, in terms of values as well as work style, trading company life remains remarkably protected and Japanese.

There are three types of trading company, as defined by the Ministry of Trade and Industry: *shōsha* (wholesale or retail enterprises conducting trade), *sōgo shōsha* (general trading companies), and *senmon shōsha* (specialty trading companies). We shall be concerned here with the *sōgo shōsha*, who manage 50 percent of all Japanese exports and 60 percent of all imports.

The worldwide information-gathering network of the larger Japanese companies rivals and exceeds all that of any organization but the United States State Department in its thoroughness. The two largest, Mitsui and Mitsubishi, send the largest portion every month overseas. There are about twelve thousand Mitsubishi Shoji employees overseas, eight thousand at home.

One might predict that within these cosmopolitan companies there would be less compartmentalization of the internationals, more unstigmatized specialization, and more efficient use of skills than in the other occupations under study. But in fact there is the same pattern of anxious jockeying for early and advantageous posts, for frequent rotations to avoid an international specialization, and for later domestic work. It may be that trading companies are so *obviously* international that employees must be more cautious: The ante is raised.

To describe better the meaning of an overseas experience for an employee of a general trading company, it is first necessary to distinguish the three types of overseas jobs available to him and the category of work each represents. Those who negotiate the sale or purchase of a special commodity such as steel or cotton are often specialists in that commodity and are sent specifically to handle that transaction. Those who are sent to manage a small office will be generalists who can oversee many kinds of work and negotiation, jacks-of-all-trades. The third type of work is top-management track, also generalist in nature. This work is done by managers in standing offices in traditionally important locations, where the manager plays a sort of undefined diplomat role. The more senior one is, the more one is assigned to generalist positions, but often these posts are in small offices of the second type, most often in developing countries.

Employees with families are sent to "better" posts but for longer terms—averaging five years overseas—while posts in developing countries are usually for two to three years. The rotations are frequent for those posted either in Japan or in developing countries, the object being "fairness and freshness"—fairness to the employee and freshness of the worker for the sake of better job performance. As in the other occupations, the location of one's post may indicate the company's assessment of one's potential and may itself affect one's future. Some overseas posts are popularly called *eriito* (elite) posts, some *deritto* (delete). As in other occupations, timing is crucial. In Mitsubishi Shoji, the largest trading company, promotions come regularly every four years. During the first two promotional grades, an employee may be sent abroad to almost any post without fearing that his career has been endangered. Work done during the third period, from the eighth to the twelfth year, however, may type a person. This is the time when it is important to be visible, to maintain good relations in the office, and therefore to avoid overseas postings. If one must be away, a career caretaker can help watch the mood in the office and keep one's name alive. In some companies this role is performed by a section chief for his subordinates. After the twelve-year mark it is especially difficult to travel and maintain a straight promotional progression since there are fewer high-status posts overseas. At this stage, employees assigned overseas sometimes leave the company, suffering a diminution in status and salary, rather than go overseas.

Overseas employees often talk about the dangers of being forgotten at home. Everyone has his favorite examples of forgotten men, or men whose "protectors" were themselves shifted out of their departments or sabotaged. For instance, a story circulating in one trading company concerned a man stationed first in Milan, then transferred to Oslo and then to Prague, who considers himself abandoned and forced to circle from mediocre post to mediocre post, never to be summoned home. Those who tell the story say that his caretaker was untrustworthy. The phrase many use in telling such stories is *tarai mawashi*, meaning "helplessly passed from one place to another." The story, with variations, appears in many companies.

Employees in the major trading companies are caught in a conflict between internationalism and protectionism. As the agents of efficient international business, the companies must use their employees in a way that produces maximum effectiveness. They have longer overseas stays, and unlike diplomats and bankers, they develop specialized skills focused on resources, production, or trade. Trading companies do attempt to protect their employees from a too-stigmatizing internationalism, as, in a wider sense, the companies protect Japan. Like other organizations, the trading companies offer predeparture orientation programs and direct and indirect financial aid to international families overseas and in Japan. The aid takes the form of hardship pay overseas and subsidies to Japanese overseas schools. They also support counseling and remedial classes in special schools in Japan and maintain dormitories for children who remain in Japan and have no appropriate relatives with whom to board. Some trading companies aid families whose children have been educated abroad by guaranteeing them future employment in liaison or translating positions. The Marubeni Company, a large diversified corporation, for example, has hired experts to advise employees about to be posted overseas concerning their children's education and publishes an in-house newsletter called "Kaigai Shijo Kyoiku News" (Overseas Children's Education News).

The trading company is seen as the go-between in Japan's international economic relationships. As such, trading companies act as international protective organizations because they do the work of exchange and—according to some observers—the real work of diplomacy and information gathering for Japan. Thus, instead of industries developing their own alliances for markets and resources, the superior information networks and efficiency of the trading companies make them logical instruments for carrying out these tasks. They act as ferryboats that have found the safest way through dangerous international currents and carry the materials of exchange back and forth—rather than as bridge builders creating a medium of exchange for others to use. Hence, it is possible that the trading companies' skill and thoroughness in acting as a buffer between domestic and foreign suppliers and markets have made genuine internationalization ultimately more difficult to accomplish in Japan.

Trading company returnees attempt to avoid career problems in several ways: First, some choose an area or commodity specialty in hopes that they may command the home office desk for that specialization, giving them at least a domestic location. Others try to choose a language or area focus that will send them to more career-enhancing locations (English, for the United States, for example). Others try hard not to specialize at all, but informants told me that this was hardest to achieve.

Outsider Internationals: Liaison and Foreign Firms

Those returnees who work for foreign or international organizations such as American-Japanese joint ventures, Japanese offices of American firms, or nongovernment agencies such as UNICEF, usually chose international work because of a prior overseas experience such as a long childhood sojourn with their families. Their attitudes range from a bitter acceptance of their outsider status to an enthusiastic, almost missionary attitude toward their international role.

Increasing numbers of returnees are hired by foreign companies in Japan, and those who work for international organizations are also predominately returnees—very often former American Field Service exchange (AFS) students or others who have had an early exposure to foreign languages or who have attended college abroad. Generally these people are not in their first jobs but have either left a Japanese company or have had previous work overseas. Using one's own initiative to find or to change a job is risky, and yet these people often have no choice, having been overseas at a stage that was crucial to their Japanese work identity. Newspaper ads reveal a wide variety of posts open to internationals. Several employment agencies specialize in finding work for returnees or for persons with international skills that are usually acquired abroad. The advertisements in English-language papers in Japan describing available candidates are revealing. Many possess quite superior educational credentials but for one reason or another are offtrack.

The overseas stays of persons in these positions are longer than those in other occupations (six to seven years, as opposed to two to three years in government or four to five years in Japanese businesses), but there is wide variation. Also, unlike employees of Japanese firms overseas, these people are not insulated in any way by their professional tasks and connections.

While these people are in Japan, they feel many of the conflicts others feel on reentry. As one executive noted, "Some Japanese become too Westernized when they live overseas. Even international companies don't want employees who are too different or unsuited to the Japanese employment system." (*Focus Japan* Aug. 1979, p. 17.) These people prefer not to be used for liaison work, which they feel delays readjustment. Highly conscious of a need to blend in, these internationals are by necessity responsible for their own careers since their jobs do not guarantee them permanent employment or automatic advancement. Even as outsiders they must be conscious of the rigidities of the mainstream system, and they must form their strategies accordingly. Several used the phrase *taido suru*, to "tide" or float with the current, balancing carefully to avoid being capsized.

The character of their work varies, but their attitudes toward the place of such work in Japan are fairly uniform and range from mild irony to bitter sarcasm. One man called his international firm a "sanatorium, a harbor for untrustworthy misfits." Another returnee who had worked for the United Nations left it because, as she wrote, it is a "vaguely floating ship, where alienated elites from developing nations attach themselves like barnacles and where everyone is a displaced person." Their ironic attitudes are reinforced by the anomie they feel in their society. They are constantly forced to be conscious of their differentness. They have chosen international work and therefore outsider status, but the degree to which they are excluded is often beyond their control. They often express dissatisfaction with the intricacies of hierarchical human relationships in Japan and say they suffer when others treat them "as if [they] were no longer one of them." One man had considerable difficulty in finding a suitable bride, since his connections in Japan were poor and his position outside most people's comprehension. He asked the foreign interviewer for names of families within the sample of internationals. While some of the returnees, especially women, feel that they have greater freedom and more opportunity in these international jobs than they would in a "Japanese" job, they regard it as the freedom of vagabondage rather than the freedom of power and status. They are burdened with an alien style and only remote connections to the home office and feel the lack of a workplace identity in which they can immerse themselves.

Writers, media employees, and others in "artistic" occupations seem to fit the category of "international and open" careers. Some of these people may have been forced out of more mainstream institutions by sidetracking, by their jet-set cosmopolitanism, or by their own frustrated ambitions. Others have deliberately chosen an environment that permits more freedom or eccentricity. Some of these offtrack people include social critics, professionals, artists, and most of the "creative underground." Nonconformist in lifestyle, they are willing to forgo more traditional kinds of status to gain a public forum or private means of self-expression, itself incompatible with a salary-man life.

Notes

Chapter 1

1. Ms. Takako Minami (in note to author, January 1987) has offered a more thorough analysis of the game and its meaning for the returnee: "Although there are different ways of singing and playing this game, according to locality, the whole chant appears to signify almost perfectly the Japanese mentality and the warning toward one who leaves a group or community for a certain purpose. He is free to leave if he has a certain purpose, but it won't be easy to return. The whole chant is:

   > Toryanse, toryanse, koko wa doko no hosomichi ja?
   > Tenjin-sama no hosomichi ja.
   > Chotto toshite kudashanse
   > Goyo no naimono toshasenu
   > Kono ko no nanatsu no oiwai ni, ofuda o osame ni mairimasu
   > Iki wa yoi, yoi, kaeri wa kowai
   > Kowai nagaramo, toryanse, toryanse.

   Tenjin-sama is a shrine dedicated to Michizane Sugawara, who rose to eminence in life by his erudition, [became] the second highest in the Imperial Court in the end of tenth century and stopped sending Japanese envoys to China in the Tung Dynasty. He also has been historically recognized as a renowned scholar of highest intelligence and has long been worshipped as *gakumon no kami*, a god of arts and sciences. *Nanatsu no oiwai* means one of the celebrations for a child of three, five, and seven years of age. The age seven is especially significant in Shintoism. A child of seven becomes eligible as a member of his community but also as a member of the broader society. *Tenjin-sama no hosomichi* may be interpreted today as a narrow path to a good experience overseas. The path to future success and prosperity based on learning overseas is narrow and may be attractive and exciting. People are allowed to take the narrow path and go abroad freely if they want, but their return is somehow frightening and [problem filled]."

2. Christie W. Kiefer suggests that the mother, in helping the child through examinations, promotes a "conversion-through-suffering" to the larger social context he will inhabit. He says that this suffering is not on a deep psychological level since there is strong continuity through the interdependence of family and school values and goals ("The Psychological Interdependence of Family, School, and Bureaucracy in Japan," *American Anthropologist* ([February 1970]: 66–75).

3. There have been other traditional sources of influence and training for the children than the family. While the family was considered the primary source of values and direction, children did receive certain kinds of education outside the home. Even a family that intended its offspring to follow in the family business would often send them as apprentices to another firm or craftsperson to learn the trade first. The family has always been considered a place of great indulgence and warmth for properly rigorous training, and rather than endanger loyalty based on this kind of warm support, the family would often choose to send a child out of the family to be "disciplined."

4. The term *mizu irazu* (water doesn't enter, or watertight) is used to describe this tight family exclusivity and privacy. *Kazoku mizuirazu ga ichiban ii* means "the close family circle is the best." By extension, any context a person calls uchi (home) is a world in which one can be excused and in which one can depend on others. These relaxed relationships cannot function if an outsider is present.

5. They entertain only rarely at their offices. If a businessman has a special bar, where he is on particulary warm terms with the bar hostess, or feels especially relaxed, he will save that place for the times when he needs solace. He will take customers or acquaintances to a more "neutral" bar rather than share the intimacy of his "home" bar with them.

Chapter 2

1. The first sojourners were elite generalists and were in a favorable position in Japanese society. Travel and foreign relations were not as such elements of a specialist career. There was competition among leaders for the opportunity to travel abroad, and "recent and frequent foreign exposure was a help, and not a handicap, in any public career" (Marius Jansen, "Modernization and Foreign Policy in Meiji Japan," in *Political Development in Modern Japan*, Robert E. Ward, ed. [Princeton, N.J.: Princeton University Press, 1968], 163).

2. See, for example, Kenneth B. Pyle, *The New Generation in Meiji Japan: Problems of Cultural Identity: 1885-1895* (Palo Alto, Calif.: Stanford University Press, 1969).

3. Jansen, "Modernization and Foreign Policy," 115. David Riesman notes the persistence of this attitude among intellectuals today:

> Whether in humility of in submerged pride, the Japanese tend ethnocentrically to think of themselves as alone in the world. . . . Japanese ethnocentrism is related to the uneasy perplexity of the Japanese intellectual as to what league he plays in. Is his an island that by accident is not located on the English Channel and happens to be in Asia, uncomfortably close to a lot of "backward" people?
> ("Japanese Intellectuals—and Americans" *American Scholar* [1964-65]: 63)

4. For further information on this and on agricultural "base-ism" *(nohonshugi)* see Gondo Seikei, quoted in Chapter 27 in *Sources of the Japanese Tradition*, Riusaka Tsunoda, William DeBary, and D. Keene, eds. (New York: Columbia University Press, 1958), 769-73; and Ronald Dore, *Land Reform in Japan* (Oxford: Oxford University Press, 1959).

5. The self-consciousness and anxiety over the higher profile which success has brought has resulted in an interesting journalistic phenomenon. In the mid-1960s, the *Nihonjinron boomu* (boom in Japanese consciousness) sparked a new dialogue in the press over what it means to be Japanese. (See Minami Hiroshi, "The Introspection Boom," *Japan Interpreter* 8 [Spring 1973].) This dialogue has tended toward discussions of Japan's place in the world but concerns itself with concrete social and cultural questions of tradition and modernization.

6. In 1974 the persons who left Japan to travel overseas on business or accompanying a family member on business were as follows:

Business	380,573
Official	10,852
At overseas branch	13,203
Diplomatic	3,973
Academic or research	5,324
Accompanying family	23,036
Total	436,961

These figures include only those who left Japan in 1974, not those already overseas. (*Japan Almanac*, Tokyo: Mainichi Shimbun, 1976.)

7. Takane Masaaki, "Readjusting to a Uniformed Society," *Japan Interpreter* 10 (Autumn 1975): 208-10.

8. Tsurumi Yoshi, "Japan" in *The Oil Crisis: The Japanese Context*, Raymond Vernon, ed. (New York: 1976), 113-27.

9. Suzanne Vogel makes the point that a housewife experiences the same pattern of apprenticeship and single commitment to her career as house-

wife that a man has to his company ("The Professional Housewife," *Japan Interpreter* 12 [Autumn 1978]: pp. 16–43).

Chapter 3

1. Shiroyama Saburo, *Mainichi ga Nichiyoobi* (Every day is Sunday), (Tokyo: Shincho Press, 1976).

2. With 566 students in its Japanese school, it is sixth largest in the world after those of Singapore, Hong Kong, Sao Paulo, Bangkok, and Djakarta.

3. *Okosama o kaigai de sodateru tame ni* (How to raise children overseas) (Tokyo: JAL Publications, annual).

4. The Hatano Family School, in Mejiro, Tokyo; see chapter 4 for more discussion.

5. Those with physical or mental handicaps or eccentricities are often "hidden" in the family. This is as much to protect that family from public embarrassment as to protect the individual: In the case of the recent Minamata pollution investigation, it was often hard to get families to admit that any of their members were victims (Norie Huddle and Michael Reich, *Island of Dreams* [New York: Autumn Press, 1975]).

6. Among the returnee families of this study, there were only two who indicated that there was a direct relationship between the overseas experience and what they see as a financial crisis. In both of these cases, the father attempted to change jobs but could not find a job for some time after returning to Japan and had to rely on contributions from kin, either parents or in-laws. After a period of several years, these fathers finally found work, but in different areas than those for which they were prepared and at some sacrifice of salary. Many people reported cases of financial disability among returnee acquaintances, but since almost all the families in the sample went overseas under the auspices of organizations guaranteeing future employment in Japan, there were few examples of real financial strain in the group.

7. Several schools have a rule that children who remain in Japan must live with a lineally connected family—that is, one that contains a grandparent of the child.

Chapter 4

1. P. A. N. Murthy, *The Rise of Modern Nationalism in Japan* (Delhi, India: Ashajanak Press, 1973).

2. In some cases, this achievement system seems more to resemble a kind

of "delayed ascription," since a child's path in some cases can be set by a very early selection, such as entrance into nursery school by examination of the mother (Ronald Dore, *The Diploma Disease: Education, Qualification and Development* [Berkeley: University of California Press, 1965], 49).

3. A national standardized examination was initiated in 1978. It is difficult to say at present if reducing the number of examinations a student takes will significantly reduce the pressure under which he or she labors. It is unlikely to stop the rapid growth of cram schools. (See Merry I. White, "Entrance Examinations," in *Encyclopedia of Japan* [Tokyo: Kodansha, 1982]).

4. *New York Times*, February 24, 1977, p. 2.

5. *Japan Times*, February 14, 1976. The newspaper report ended on this understated note: "The woman was a PTA official and was enthusiastic about her son's education."

6. *Boston Globe*, May 22, 1975.

7. *New York Times*, July 29, 1979. In the first half of 1979, 521 children between the ages of twelve and twenty took their own lives (seventy more than the year before). The causes of juvenile suicide given by the Ministry of Education include "pessimism over examinations, poor job prospects and poor performance in school." It should be noted that the rate of juvenile suicide for those between the ages fifteen and nineteen is higher in the United States than in Japan, contrary to American popular opinion (Merry I. White, *The Japanese Educational Challenge: A Commitment to Children* [New York: Free Press], 137).

8. The coaching schools (juku), which many see as necessary in preparing their children for the examinations, are often intensely competitive and themselves very selective. These schools are experiencing a significant boom. In a 1976 series in the *Mainichi Shimbun*, it was estimated that there are from seventy thousand to one hundred thousand of these private after-school schools, for children from elementary through high school. There are two major types of juku: examination-oriented *(shingaku juku)* and supplementary *(gakushu juku)*.

It is estimated that nationwide, one of every three primary school students and one of every two junior high school students attend these juku but in Tokyo there is over 80 percent attendance in these age groups. The schools have been so successful in encouraging parents to enroll their children that there has evolved a sideline examination system for entrance into the top juku. New lucrative franchises of juku have appeared. One, based in Nagoya, has six hundred branches; another in Tokyo has branches at many suburban train termini. Juku are not at present under the control of the Ministry of Education, and it is claimed that here are many abuses as well as many substandard classroom facilities.

Furukawa Noboru, who has established a chain of juku (he is called the "king of juku") says that juku are necessary to bridge the gap of present-day realities in Japan. According to Furukawa, public schools do not face the fact of competition, and ignoring facts will not help the children: "I hope pupils will develop 'fighting spirits' through their attendance at juku to be able to meet the harsh challenge of reality as they face it today and in the future'" (*Japan Times*, May 9, 1979, p. 9).

9. In 1976 a high school teacher was finally acquitted after seven years of court battles over his receiving money for after-school tutoring. A high court ultimately decided that the payments (of about four hundred dollars) were permissible as "within the bounds of social etiquette" (*Japan Times*, March 15, 1976). The Teachers' Union also contributed to the bifurcation by insisting that tutoring by teachers often led to exploitation and that parents took advantage of already hardworking teachers.

10. It is clear that the extra day of a five-day school week would be swallowed up by juku. Parents object to the reduction, saying that the child's education on the holiday would then be the mother's responsibility. The time must always be *directed* time; as one editorial said, "Children cannot just be let loose, unattended by anyone" ("No more Cramming," *Japan Quarterly* 19 [October–December 1972]: 397).

11. The Ministry of Education directs curricula, approves textbooks, and generally supervises all aspects of education. Other functions include the drafting of educational bills and preparation of the departmental budget for the Diet, the establishment of surveys and research institutes, and the supervision of museums and grants. Under the minister, who is a political appointee, and his advisers there are five bureaus: elementary and secondary education, higher education, social (adult) education, physical education, and administration. The most important advisory committee is the Liberal Democratic Party's Educational Committee, on which all previous ministers and many senior Diet members sit and that is said to be a powerful conservative influence on Japanese education.

12. Ronald Dore, *Education in Tokugawa Japan* (Berkeley: University of California Press, 1965) 170.

13. These views were extracted from reports and publications of the Ministry of Education or affiliated research bodies. These were written to advise parents, teachers, and policymakers on the procedures for dealing with returnee children.

14. *Kaigai Shijo Kyoiku no suido ni kansuru konponteki shisaku ni tsuite* (Concerning the basic policy toward the education of overseas children) (Tokyo: Ministry of Education, April 1976).

15. *Kaigai Zaikin no kata no Shijo no Kyoiku ni tsuite* (Concerning the education of children of those employed overseas) (Tokyo: Keimei Gakuen, 1975).

16. This statement is often made by returning university students who say that having to cope with anomie and the problems of taking care of themselves overseas made them able to cope and yet sometimes too aggressive in Japan.

17. These remarks were taken from conversations with Mr. S. Ogiyama, a counselor of the foundation (and a retired Ministry of Education bureaucrat) and from his book, *Umi o Wataru Kodomotachi* (Children who cross the seas) (Tokyo, Foundation for the Education of Children Overseas, 1976).

18. The foundation publishes a monthly magazine, *Kaigai Shijo Kyoiku*, featuring an extensive discussion of Japanese overseas education and including articles by overseas parents. Its regular advertisers are *juku*, correspondence courses, and companies selling tapes and texts to overseas children.

19. Although not a member of the group, Nagai Michio, a former Minister of Education, advocated what he calls "expansive international education in Japan and reentry education designed to maintain rather than eliminate the effects of an overseas experience" (*Look Japan* [April 1976]).

20. The Teachers' Union especially condemns the expenditure of public funds on the children of these people, calling it payment for "elite remedial education." The conflict between those who advocate readjustment and those who hope to internationalize the educational system is supported by the polarized antipathy between the Teachers' Union and the ministry. Thomas Rohlen ("Is Japanese Education Becoming Less Egalitarian?" *Journal of Japanese Studies* [Winter 1976-77]: 37-70) has observed the contrasts in ideology in Japanese education in the debate between the ministry and the Teachers' Union. After World War II, the teachers' union (Nikkyoso) was established as a left-wing protest against low salaries and governmental lack of interest in the problems of teachers. The union's second-order priorities involve the style and content of education. The union hopes to achieve "the democratization of academic study and research, and ... the construction of democratic education" (Article 7 of the union rules, quoted in Ronald S. Anderson, Japan: Three Epochs of Modern Education [Washington, D.C.: United States Department of Health, Education, and Welfare, 1975], 238). The main force of union activity, however, has been in opposition to the Ministry of Education, and primarily to organize labor against management. The ministry has made strategic moves to control curriculum, screen texts, rate teacher efficiency, administer achievement tests, and establish the morals course, and all of these are seen as aggrandizing and aggressive by the Teachers' Union. Any move on the part of the ministry to establish a program on its own is met with suspicion by the Teachers' Union. The overseas and reentry programs are not staffed by teachers or administrators with active union connections, but rather from the pool of retirees

and teachers from remote areas of Japan. This policy is seen by the union as a strategy to isolate the returnee and overseas education from the mainstream of education, and to eliminate sources of dissidence.

21. *Kaigai Shijo Kyoiku*, Ministry of Education Report.

22. Teachers are sent for two-to-three-year postings to overseas schools. They are on special leave from the prefectures, who pay their salaries. The rapid turnover is seen to be good for morale and "freshness" as well as assuring that overseas children will be learning a "real" Japanese curriculum and experiencing an uncontaminated Japanese teaching style.

23. The need to place bureaucrats in suitable jobs after their retirement at age fifty-five is one shared by all ministries, but the Ministry of Education has had no regular pattern of "falling from heaven" *(amakudari)* postretirement placement in the private sector. Some retired teachers and administrators do have jobs in private education—most notably in the burgeoning juku discussed above, but it is difficult to find suitable outside employment for regular ministry bureaucrats. The ministry has welcomed the opportunity to provide a roof over the heads of its retired employees through the development of overseas education, and consequently overseas school administrators are often older bureaucrats with little training and little professional experience in the special problems of overseas Japanese children.

24. Companies sometimes give tuition support for their employees' children who attend private receiving or cooperating schools. Other companies help by contributing directly to the schools, who then give tuition reductions to the employees of those companies.

25. In September 1977, as the result of a cooperative effort between International Christian University and the Ministry of Education, a new private high school to accommodate returnees was established at International Christian University. The intention was to integrate returnees with "general students." There were 240 pupils in the beginning class, 160 of whom were returnees. The former submit only essays as a test for admission, whereas the latter sit for examinations. Three hundred million of the 1.2 billion yen the school cost were donated by the Ministry of Education–about 25 percent.

26. Flower-arranging classes and gymnastics academies are also included in this category.

27. Akira Hoshino, "An Elaboration of the 'Culture Shock' Phenomenon: Problems of Japanese Youth Returning from Overseas." In *Uprooting and Surviving*, R. C. Nann, ed. (D. Reidel, 1982).

28. In *Kaigai Shijo Kyoiku* (the 1976 ministry report), the following distribution of returnee children among private schools in "receiving facilities" was given.

RETURNEE CHILDREN IN PRIVATE RECEIVING SCHOOLS, 1976

	First Year	*Second Year*	*Third Year*
Middle school: 136 (100%)	37 (27%)	37 (27%)	62 (46%)
(32% of total)			
High school: 291 (100%)	94 (32%)	112 (39%)	85 (29%)
(68% of total)			
Total number of students:			
427			
(100%)			

RETURNEE CHILDREN BY AGE GROUP, 1976	
Middle school	3,270 (71%)
High school	1,314 (29%)
Total	4,584 (100%)

29. October 1975, at the Family School, Mejiro, Tokyo.

30. There has been a marked split among parents in their views of the overseas experience between what a teacher at one overseas school called the "internationals" and the "real Japanese." Most parents who use the overseas schools, like the parents who use juku in Japan, do not use them as alternative education but as extra education to buttress their children's chances in the mainstream. These parents are heavily committed to the goals and values of the Japanese system and rarely express much active interest in alternatives.

The overseas schools and returnee schools, too, serve the needs of mainstream aspirants and are used by persons who are anxious that their children not be marked as outsiders. The returnee schools, like juku, support the existing framework of Japanese education by isolating potential problems of dysfunction. The so-called international parents on the other hand, see the overseas experience and the "crisis of return" as chances for change in the educational system. The parents who want their children to have a non-Japanese life overseas feel that Japanese schools abroad should maintain language ability but not isolate children from the new environment. They also want their children to go to "regular" schools in Japan, not isolated from other children, but they want the schools to admit them without drastic reprocessing and to incorporate a more broadly flexible curriculum. There are few, however, who opt for a totally nonmainstream education for their children. In this Japanese parents are like some American parents who want change in the public school system but who hesitate to enroll their own children to gain a foothold in the system. Of the Japanese parents, it has been said: "Their leftist perspective leads them to public criticism but privately they remain anxious that their own ... status (gained of course through elite education) be replicated by their children through their success in school" (Rohlen, "Is Japanese Education Becoming Less Egalitarian?" 43n.).

31. Sato Yoshiko, "Facing Silent Society: The Maladjustment of Japanese Returning Children" (Harvard Graduate School of Education, 1982), 23.

32. Ibid., 29.

33. Ibid. p. 29

34. *Mainichi Shimbun*, February 2, 1977, p. 15.

35. Ibid.

36. For families from *shitamachi* (downtown) areas and backgrounds, the experience is somewhat different. One returnee family noticed that their children had particular handicaps. In the ordinary public schools of shitamachi areas, even though children are prepared for entrance examinations to universities, traditional merchant skills are emphasized—such as the use of the abacus, bookkeeping, and calligraphy. The overseas sojourn made these children different from their shitamachi friends, and their families decided to send them to private readjustment schools where, although the shitamachi skills might be ignored, the equalizing examination skills would not be. (See Ronald Dore, *City Life in Japan* [Berkeley: University of California Press, 1958], 11–14, for a description of the traditional skills of shitamachi.)

Chapter 5

1. Suzanne Vogel, "Toward Understanding the Adjustment Problems of Foreign Families in the College Community" (Harvard University Health Service, 1985).

2. According to a report in the *Shukan Bunshin*, December 15, 1975, the incidence of divorce among returnees is increasing and is particularly high among couples who have been stationed in Southeast Asia. The magazine attributes these divorces to the readjustment problems of wives "who get used to the affluent life made possible by the low wages of household help [and] lose interest in keeping house.... On return to Japan, they find they must ... do all the chores and look after the children ... and marital fights follow which lead to a split." No separation or

divorce appeared in the group under study, but the number of returnees from such postings in the sample is quite small. Women themselves did not attribute postreturn marital problems to having been "spoiled" overseas, nor did they claim that there were such problems as mentioned in the above article.

3. Notes from a workshop held by Pola Cosmetic Company, Tokyo 1976, attended by the author; the workshop was a follow-up to a survey conducted by Pola.

4. The description of work organization and individual careers are based in a model that flourished in the early 1970s, before the energy crisis created a new economic environment, provoking new organizational strategies. Although these new strategies (see Thomas P. Rohlen, "'Permanent Employment' Faces Recession, Slow Growth and an Aging Work Force," *Journal of Japanese Studies* 5, [Summer 1979]: 235–72) may eventually produce change in the international sector of Japanese business, it is in fact the lag in redefinition of work in this sector that causes some of the problems for Japanese employed abroad.

5. *New York Times*, March 18, 1985, p. D8.

6. Takeo Naruse, "Are the Japanese Workaholics?" *Look Japan* (July 10, 1979):

7. It is well-known that the most intense study takes place in high school and that after admission to university many students take advantage of their new freedom. Even at the most prestigious universities, class cutting for maj-jongg and coffee is frequent.

8. Students polled in 1976 said that they favored the largest and strongest companies. Few in the survey chose companies on the basis of "work they truly enjoy" or "jobs which permit them to exhibit their capacities to the fullest" (*Journal of the American Chamber of Commerce in Japan* 13, [June 5, 1976]).

9. On socialization to the work group, see Thomas Rohlen, *For Harmony and Strength* (Berkeley: University of California Press, 1974).

10. Robert Bellah, *Tokugawa Religion* (Chicago: Free Press, 1957), 16.

11. There may, however, be serious problems if a younger employee becomes the superior of an older. A well-publicized murder in 1978 was said to have been based on such a situation. The older simply could not use the polite address demanded of the relationship (Toshi Kii, "Status Changes of Japanese Elderly in Legal, Family and Economic Institutions" [Presentation to the Annual Meeting of the American Sociological Association, University of Georgia, August 1979]).

12. Hayao Kawai, "Egalitarianism in Japanese Education," *Japan Echo*, 2 (1975): 27.

13. Thomas P. Rohlen, "The Company Work Group," in *Modern Japanese Organization and Decision Making*, Ezra F. Vogel, ed. (Berkeley: University of California Press, 1975), 185–209.

14. "One of the striking characteristics of the Japanese collectivity orientation is the strong suspicion that the group feels toward outsiders. . . . Mid-career recruits tend to be looked upon as 'quasi-outsiders' and they are frequently treated with a certain amount of suspicion" (M. Y. Yoshino, *Japan's Managerial System* [Cambridge: MIT Press, 1968], 232).

15. See C. K. Yang, "Chinese Bureaucratic Behavior," *Confucianism in Action*, David S. Nivison and Arthur Wright, eds. (Palo Alto, Calif.: Stanford University Press, 1959).

16. A distinction should be made between the mainstream leader who leads by means of his position and by manipulation of human relationships and the charismatic leaders in business who are cast in a more "heroic mold" and provide energetic highly personalized models, such as Matsushita, Honda, and Morita, of Matsushita Electric, Honda, and Sony, respectively.

17. The recent recession has meant that companies sometimes shift some workers to related plants. In these moves, to avoid the difficult shift of loyalty and identity, the shifted worker will continue to wear his first company's uniform and will act as an "emissary" from the first plant (T. Rohlen, " 'Permanent Employment' ").

18. John Bennett, Herbert Passin, and Robert McKnight, *In Search of Identity* (Minneapolis: University of Minnesota Press, 1958), 70.

19. There are, however, some domestic specialist jobs that may lead to permanent sidetracking as "international"—recently, companies have not been restraining those whose skills as specialists have become obsolete through the advance of technology, and some of these people are instead being sent overseas. One man, an accountant with Toyota, was sent to a small branch office in South America when his job in Japan was made obsolete by computerization. He feels that he will never be able to settle in Japan permanently, except as a *benriya* ("convenience person," usually a translator in this situation) with liaison skills.

20. Ronald Anderson, *Education in Japan* (Washington, D.C.: U.S. Superintendent of Documents, 1974), 185–87.

21. Harumi Befu, "Power in the Great White Tower" (Paper presented at the Annual Meeting of the American Association for the Advancement of Science, February 25, 1974).

22. Private correspondence with a former teacher of the returnee.

23. It is now common for career bankers to take language training even after their initial five-year apprenticeship. The language is usually English, but

personnel directors are trying to encourage them to take such specialty languages (meaning non-English languages) as Arabic or German.

24. In one major bank, two-thirds of all returnees in Tokyo were at international desks.

25. Bennett, Passin, and McKnight divided their sample of Japanese overseas students into two groups on the basis of their overseas "styles": constrictors and adjusters. I borrow the latter term for my middle group, using it for return rather than overseas behavior, and suggest a slightly wider range of possibilities than his group showed (*In Search of Identity*, 181).

26. Bennett, Passin, and McKnight, *In Search of Identify*, 189. The authors' "constrictor" pattern for overseas Japanese students is interesting here. However, their model shows this group as resistant to Americanization and reluctant to see differentness or change in customs or style. Their sample shows very Japanese behavior and conservative outlook, as does mine. Members of both groups showed both a highly involved attachment to the overseas experience, sensitivity to the differences between cultures, and a strong consciousness of the need to conform to a well-defined set of norms (181).

Chapter 6

1. Other studies of group membership and boundaries include Fredrik Barth, *Ethnic Groups and Boundaries* (Boston: Little, Brown, 1969); Mary Douglas, *Purity and Danger* (London: Penguin, 1966); Rosabeth M. Kanter, *Commitment and Community* (Cambridge, Mass.: Harvard University Press, 1972); Kai Erikson, *The Wayward Puritans* (New York: Wiley, 1966).

2. In discussing Etzioni's compliance model, Howard Aldrich puts this another way, saying that the type of compliance (normative, utilitarian, or coercive) that determines membership in an organization determines the organization's ability to arrange its boundaries—that the coercive type has the most control of the boundaries and the normative, least control ("Organizational Boundaries and Interorganizational Conflict," *Human Relations* 24 [1971]: 279–83).

3. Karl Deutsch, investigating the types of belonging that tie an individual to the state, makes a useful distinction when he discusses the difference between group membership, in which *active* participation is a requirement *(politai)* and the *symbolic* identity *(patriotai)*, which he says is a characteristic of nationalism. The first, politai, represents membership in a group of any size in which a member's activities can be directly tied to the purposes and values of the group. This kind of membership can be

called "contractual" or "interactional," depending on whether the activity or the locus and relationships involved in the activity are more important. It might be said that in many modern nation-states the moments when a person engages in active participation as a citizen are few: Serving in the military forces or voting seem to be today's only ties to national concerns. The major source of identity as citizen is symbolic—Deutsch's *patriotai*. This type of belonging is rarely evoked in everyday life and is in many cases residual. In a group without politically determined boundaries, it may be called "ideological ethnicity" and may in such cases serve as a strong point of cohesion, as for instance, among exiles or émigrés (*Political Community at the International Level* [Princeton, N.J.: Princeton University Press, 1953].)

4. Takeo Doi, *The Anatomy of Dependence* (Tokyo: Kodansha, 1975).

5. Robert J. Smith, "The Japanese Rural Community: Norms, Sanctions and Ostracism," *American Anthropologist* 1 (1961): 522–33.

6. The extent to which a society is "plural" does not necessarily indicate the extent to which individuals can be "plural" in their memberships.

7. Bruce La Brack calls this a tribal model of identity, in which only Japanese are real humans and everyone else is a *yosomono* (outsider). ("Internationalization: An Anti-Japanese Activity," *Japan Times*, August 7, 1983, p. 12).

8. For descriptions of other types of cultural brokers see George Simmel, "The Sociological Significance of the Stranger" in *Introduction to the Science of Sociology*, R. E. Park, ed., (Chicago: University of Chicago Press, 1921), 322; Edward M. Bruner, "Primary Group Experience and the Processes of Acculturation," *American Anthropologist* 58, (1956): 612.

9. Mark Zimmerman, *How to Do Business with the Japanese*, (New York: Random House, 1985), 13.

10. A Japanese scholar in Delhi half-jokingly referred to the need in Japan for a Shinto repurification rite for overseas returnees, which he felt could take care of their problem very simply. Rosabeth Kanter described the rituals of the Oneida community, which regarded the outside world as deviant and polluting: "For members who traveled outside, there was a criticism before they left to provide 'sustaining power from the heart of the family' for the ordeal, and one on their return, 'to relieve them of spiritual contamination'" (*Commitment and Community*, 198). After visitors left, the community had a "ritual cleaning bee" to remove uncleanliness. Japanese overseas sojourners report a predeparture informal warning preparation by kin and friends, and a debriefing on return that, though not formalized, may serve the same function as those of the Oneida community.

11. Kai Erikson describes this function of deviance: "Deviant behavior is not

not a simple kind of leakage which occurs when the machinery of society is in poor working order, but may be, in controlled quantities, an important condition for preserving the stability of social life. Deviant forms of behavior, by marking the outer edges of group life, give the inner structure its special character and thus supply the framework within which the people of the group develop an orderly sense of their own cultural identity" (*The Wayward Puritans*, 13).

Boundaries, according to Erikson, regulate the amount and type of deviation in any society. But they also emphasize group identity in two important ways. First, as Erikson points out, is the reinforcement of acceptable cultural traits and the establishment of a model of group belonging relevant to the contrasts and interactions of the border. The other, which is more important to the present study, is the function of distinguishing active members from inactive or deviant ones. A broker may thus be an outsider before he gets to the boundary. Groups may send some of their members to the border because of prior "deviance" while scapegoating those who are accidental border figures for the differentness they have acquired by their positions on the margins.

Bibliography

Books

Anderson, Ronald S. *Japan, Three Epochs of Modern Education*. Washington, D.C.: United States Department of Health, Education, and Welfare, 1959

Aso, M., and I. Amano, *Education and Japan's Modernization*. Tokyo: Ministry of Foreign Affairs, 1972.

Austin, Lewis, ed. *Japan: The Paradox of Progress*. New Haven, Conn.: Yale University Press, 1976.

Barth, Fredrik. *Ethnic Groups and Boundaries*. Boston: Little, Brown, 1969.

Bell, Wendell, and Walter E. Freeman, eds. *Ethnicity and Nation-building: Comparative, International and Historical Perspectives*. Beverly Hills, Calif.: Sage Publications, 1974.

Bellah, Robert N. *Tokugawa Religion*. Chicago: Free Press, 1957.

Bendix, Reinhard, and Seymour Martin Lipset. *Class, Status and Power: Social Stratification in Comparative Perspective*. Glencoe, Ill.: Free Press, 1966.

Bennett, John W., Herbert Passin, and Robert K. McKnight. *In Search of Identity*. Minneapolis: University of Minnesota Press, 1958.

Blalock, H. M. *Toward a Theory of Minority Group Relations*. New York: John Wiley & Sons, 1967.

Campbell, Ernest Q., ed. *Racial Tensions and National Identity*. Nashville, Tenn.: Vanderbilt University, 1972.

Cohen, Abner. *Two-Dimensional Man*. Berkeley: University of California Press, 1974.

161

Cole, Robert E. Japanese Blue Collar: *The Changing Tradition.* Berkeley: University of California Press, 1971.

Confucius. *The Analects.* Trans. Arthur Waley. London: G. Allen & Unwin, 1938.

Coughlin, Richard. *Double Identity: The Chinese in Modern Thailand.* London: Oxford University Press, 1960.

Cox, Oliver C. *Caste, Class and Race: A Study in Social Dynamics.* New York: Monthly Review Press, 1959.

Dahrendorf, Ralf. *Class and Class Conflict in Industrial Society.* Palo Alto: Stanford University Press, 1959.

―――. *Life Chances.* Chicago: University of Chicago Press, 1978.

Deutsch, Karl. *Political Community at the International Level.* Princeton, N.J.: Princeton University Press, 1953.

DeVos, George. *Socialization for Achievement.* Berkeley: University of California Press, 1973.

―――. *Reponses to Change.* New York: Van Nostrand, 1975.

DeVos, George, and Lola Romanucci-Ross. *Ethnic Identity, Cultural Continuities and Change.* Palo Alto, Calif.: Mayfield Publications, 1975.

DeVos, George, and Hiroshi Wagatsuma. *Japan's Invisible Race: Caste in Culture and Personality.* Berkeley: University of California Press, 1972.

Doi, Takeo. *The Anatomy of Dependence.* Tokyo: Kodansha, 1975.

Dore, Ronald. *City Life in Japan.* Berkeley: University of California Press, 1958.

―――. *Land Reform in Japan.* Oxford: Oxford University Press, 1959.

―――. *Education in Tokugawa Japan.* Berkeley: University of California Press, 1965.

―――. *The Diploma Disease: Education, Qualification and Development.* Berkeley: University of California Press, 1976.

Douglas, Mary. *Purity and Danger.* London: Penguin, 1966.

Duijker, H. C. J., and N. H. Frijda. *National Character and National Stereotypes.* Amsterdam: North Holland Publishing Co., 1960.

Dumont, Louis. *Homo Hierarchicus.* Chicago: University of Chicago Press, 1970.

Embree, John F. *Suye Mura.* Chicago: University of Chicago Press, 1939.

Enloe, Cynthia. *Ethnic Conflict and Political Identity.* Boston: Little, Brown, 1973.

Erikson, Eric. *Childhood and Society.* New York: Norton, 1963.

―――. *Identity, Youth and Crisis.* New York: Norton, 1968.

Erikson, Kai T. *Wayward Puritans: A Study in the Sociology of Deviance.* New York: John Wiley & Sons, 1966.

Fallers, Lloyd A. *The Social Anthropology of the Nation-State*. Chicago: University of Chicago Press, 1974.

Freud, Sigmund. *Group Psychology and the Analysis of the Ego*. New York: Norton, 1969.

Fukuzawa, Yukichi. *Autobiography*. New York: Columbia University Press, 1966.

Geertz, Clifford, ed. *Old Societies and New States*. Glencoe, Ill.: Free Press, 1963.

Glazer, Nathan, and D. P. Moynihan. *Ethnicity: Theory and Experience*. Cambridge, Mass.: Harvard University Press, 1975.

Goffman, Erving. *Stigma: Notes on the Management of Spoiled Identity*. Englewood Cliffs, N.J.: Prentice-Hall, 1963.

Gordon, Milton M. *Assimilation in American Life: Role of Race, Religion and National Origins*. New York: Oxford University Press, 1964.

Guetzkow, H. *Multiple Loyalties*. Princeton, N.J.: Princeton University Press, 1955.

Hasegawa, Nyozekan. *The Japanese Character*. Tokyo: Kodansha, 1966.

Hollerman, Leon. *Japan's Dependence on the World Economy*. Princeton, N.J.: Princeton University Press, 1967.

Holloman, Regina E. "Ethnic Boundary Maintenance, Readaptation and Societal Evolution in the San Blas Islands of Panama." In *Ethnicity and Resource Competition in Plural Societies*, ed. Leon Despres. The Hague: Mouton, 1975.

Huddle, Norie, and Michael Reich. *Island of Dreams*. New York: Autumn Press, 1975.

Iriye, Akira. *Across the Pacific*. New York: Harcourt, Brace & World, 1967.

———. *Mutual Images*. Cambridge, Mass.: Harvard University Press, 1975.

Isaacs, Harold. *Images of Asia*. New York: Harper & Row, 1972.

———. *Idols of the Tribe*. New York: Harper & Row, 1975.

Ishida, Eiichiro. *Japanese Culture*. Honolulu: University of Hawaii Press, 1974.

Japan Foundation. *Report on Overseas Japanese Education*. November 1975.

Joseph, Bernard. *Nationality: Its Nature and Problems*. New Haven, Conn.: Yale University Press, 1929.

Kaigo, Tokiomi. *Japanese Education: Its Past and Present*. Tokyo: Kokusai Bunka Shinkokai, 1968.

Kanter, Rosabeth M. *Commitment and Community*. Cambridge, Mass.: Harvard University Press, 1972.

Keene, Donald. *The Japanese Discovery of Europe*. New York: Grove Press, 1954.

Kelman, Herbert C. *International Behavior: A Social-Psychological Analysis.* New York: Holt, Rinehart and Winston, 1965.

Kelman, Herbert C., and Raphael S. Ezekiel. *Cross-National Encounters.* San Francisco: Jossey-Bass, 1970.

Kitamura, Hiroshi. "Psychological Dimensions of U.S.–Japanese Affairs," *Occasional Papers in International Affairs,* 28, August 1971.

Kluckhohn, Clyde, and Henry A. Murray, eds. *Personality in Nature, Society and Culture.* New York: Alfred A. Knopf, 1967.

Kobayashi, Tetsuya. *Society, Schools and Progress in Japan.* Oxford: Pergamon Press, 1976.

Kojima, Gunzo. *The Philosophical Foundations for Democratic Education in Japan.* Tokyo: International Christian University, 1959.

Lambert, R. D., and O. Klineberg. *Children's Views of Foreign Peoples.* New York: Appleton-Century-Crofts, 1967.

Lebra, William P., and Takie Lebra, eds. *Japanese Culture and Behavior.* Honolulu: University of Hawaii Press, 1974.

LeVine, Robert and Donald T. Campbell. *Ethnocentrism: Theories of Conflict, Ethnic Attitudes and Group Behavior.* New York: John Wiley & Sons, 1972.

Linton, Ralph. *The Cultural Background of Personality.* New York: Appleton-Century, 1945.

MacGregor, Gordon. *American Fulbright Scholars.* Ithaca, N.Y.: Cornell University Press, 1962.

Mainichi, Shimbum. *Japan Almanac* Tokyo, 1976.

Maruyama, Masao. *Thought and Behavior in Modern Japanese Politics.* Oxford: Oxford University Press, 1963.

Metraux, Guy S. *Exchange of Persons: The Evolution of Cross-Cultural Education.* New York: Social Sciences Research Council, 1952.

Ministry of Education. *The Role of Education in the National and Economic Development of Japan.* Tokyo: Japanese National Commission for UNESCO, 1966.

———. *Education in Japan.* Tokyo, 1971.

Morley, James W. *Dilemmas of Growth in Pre-War Japan.* Princeton, N.J.: Princeton University Press, 1971.

Morris, R. *The Two-Way Mirror.* Minneapolis: University of Minnesota Press, 1960.

Murthy, P. A. Narasimha. *The Rise of Modern Nationalism in Japan.* Delhi: Ashajanak Press, 1973.

Nagai, Michio. *Higher Education in Japan: Its Take-Off and Crash.* Tokyo: University of Tokyo Press, 1971.

Nakagawa, Hideyasu. *Report to Nagai Michio on Education of Overseas Japanese Children.* Tokyo: Ministry of Education, 1975.

Nakane, Chie. *Japanese Society.* Berkeley: University of California Press, 1970.

Nakaya, Kenichi, and Robert S. Schwantes. *Ten Years of Cultural and Educational Exchange between Japan and America, 1952–1961: A Report Submitted to the Joint U.S.–Japan Conference on Cultural and Educational Exchange.* Tokyo: United States Embassy, 1962.

Organization for Economic Cooperation and Development. *Reviews of National Policies for Education: Japan.* Paris: OECD, 1973.

———. *Education Policy and Planning in Japan.* Paris: OECD, 1973.

Passin, Herbert. *Society and Educaton in Japan.* New York: Teachers College Press, Columbia University, 1965.

Pyle, Kenneth B. *The New Generation in Meiji Japan: Problems of Cultural Identity 1885–1895.* Palo Alto, Calif.: Stanford University Press, 1969.

Reischauer, E. O. *Toward the Twenty-first Century: Education for a Changing World.* New York: Alfred A. Knopf. 1974.

Rohlen, Thomas P. *For Harmony and Strength.* Berkeley: University of California Press, 1974.

Scanlon, David G., and James J. Shields, eds. *Problems and Prospects in International Education.* New York: Teachers College Press, Columbia University, 1968.

Schermerhorn, R. A. *Comparative Ethnic Relations: A Framework for Theory and Research.* New York: Random House, 1970.

Schwantes, Robert S. *Japanese and Americans: A Century of Cultural Relations.* Westport, Conn.: Greenwood Press, 1976.

Singleton, John. *Nichuu, A Japanese School.* New York: Holt, Rinehart & Winston, 1967.

Strauss, Anselm. *Mirrors and Masks: The Search for Identity.* Glencoe, Ill.: Free Press, 1959.

Tsunoda, Riusaka, William DeBary, and D. Keene. *Sources of the Japanese Tradition.* New York: Columbia University Press, 1958.

Tsurumi, Yoshi. *The Japanese are Coming.* Cambridge, Mass.: MIT Press, 1976.

U.S. Department of State. *Cross-Cultural Education: A Bibliography of Government-Sponsored and Private Research on Foreign Students and Trainees in the United States and other countries 1946–1964.* Washington, D.C.: Government Printing Office, 1965.

Van den Berghe, Pierre L. *Race and Racism: A Comparative Perspective.* New York: John Wiley & Sons, 1967.

———. *Race and Ethnicity: Essays in Comparative Sociology.* New York: Basic Books, 1970.

Vogel, Ezra F. *Japan's New Middle Class.* Berkeley: University of California Press, 1963.

———, ed. *Modern Japanese Organization and Decision-Making.* Berkeley: University of California Press, 1975.

Ward, Robert Edward. *Political Development in Modern Japan.* Princeton N.J.: Princeton University Press, 1968.

Watson, Jeanne, and Ronald Lippitt. *Learning Across Cultures.* Ann Arbor: University of Michigan Press, 1955.

Weber, Max. *Economy and Society.* New York: Bedminster, 1968.

White, Merry I. *The Japanese Educational Challenge: A Commitment to Children.* New York: Free Press, 1987.

Yoshino, M. Y. *Japan's Managerial System: Tradition and Innovation.* Cambridge, Mass.: MIT Press, 1968.

Articles

Abrams, Arnold. "The Problems of Mixed Marriages: Crossing Cultures in Japan." *New Leader,* June 24, 1974, 11–12.

Adams, Donald, and Robert Bjork. "Modernization as Affected by Governmental and International Educational Influences: Japan." In *Governmental Policy and International Education,* ed. S. Fraser. New York: John Wiley & Sons, 1965.

Aldrich, Howard. "Organizational Boundaries and Interorganizational Conflict." *Human Relations* 24 (1971): 279–93.

American Chamber of Commerce in Japan. "Japanese University Graduates Favor Companies Noted for 'Stability' and 'Good Working Conditions.'" *Journal of the ACCJ* 13 (1976).

Befu, Harumi. "Power in the Great White Tower." Paper presented at the annual meeting of the American Association for Advancement of Science, February 25, 1974.

Bennett, John W. "Innovative Potential of American-Educated Japanese." *Human Organization* 21 (Winter 1962–63): 246–51.

Bierstedt, A. "The Sociology of Majorities." *American Social Review* 13 (December 1948): 700–710.

Bruner, E. M. "Primary Group Experience and the Process of Acculturation." *American Anthropologist* 58 (1956): 605–623.

Bruner, J. S., and H. V. Perlmutter. "Compatriot, Foreigner: A Study of

Impressions Formation in Three Countries." *Journal of Abnormal and Social Psychology* 55 (1957): 253–60.

Campbell, D. T. and R. A. LeVine. "A Proposal for Cooperative Cross-cultural Research on Ethnocentrism." *Journal of Conflict Resolution* 5 (1961): 82–108.

Caudill, William, and Harry Scarr. "Japanese Value Orientations and Culture Change." *Ethnology* 1 (1962): 53–91.

Coelho, G. V. "Impacts of Studying Abroad." *Journal of Social Issues* 18 (1) (1962).

DeVos, George. "Japan's International Future: Cultural Dilemmas in Citizenship and Social Belonging." Proceedings of the Second Tsukuba International Symposium on the Role of Japan in the Future World, Tsukuba, December 1975.

Deutsch, S. E., and G. Won. "Some Factors in the Adjustment of Foreign Nationals in the U.S." *Journal of Social Issues* 19 (1963): 115–22.

DuBois, Cora. "Some Notions on Learning Intercultural Understanding." In *Education and Anthropology,* ed. George Spindler, 89–126. Stanford: Stanford University Press, 1955.

"Education Animal." *Japan Quarterly* 19 (January–March 1972):

Embree, John. "Standardized Error and Japanese Character." *World Politics* 2 (April 1950): 439–443.

Encyclopedia of the Social Sciences (1931), v. "ethnocentrism."

Fishman, Joshua A. "Language and Ethnicity." *Language, Ethnicity and Intergroup Relations.* 15–57. London: Academic Press, 1977.

Francis, E. K. "The Nature of the Ethnic Group." *American Journal of Sociology* 52 (1947): 393–400.

Glaser, Daniel. "Dynamics of Ethnic Identification." *American Sociological Review* 23 (1958): 31–40.

Glazer, Nathan. "There Are No Drop-Outs in Japan: The Japanese Educational System." *Asia's New Grant,* ed. Hugh Patrick and Henry Rosovsky. Washington, D.C.: The Brookings Institute, 1976.

Gorer, Geoffrey. "The Concept of National Character." In Clyde Kluckhohn and Henry A. Murray, *Personality in Nature, Society and Culture,* 246–59. New York: Alfred A. Knopf, 1967.

———. "National Character: Theory and Practice." In *The Study of Culture at a Distance,* ed. Margaret Mead and Rhoda Metraux, 57–82. Chicago: University of Chicago, 1953.

Haglund, Elaine Jean. "Awareness in Japanese Education of Japan's Dependence upon Foreign Resources." Ph.D. diss., Michigan State University, 1972.

Hechter, Michael. "Towards a Theory of Ethnic Change." *Politics and Society* (Fall 1971): 21–45.

Higuchi, Keiko. "The PTA—A Channel for Political Activism." *Japan Interpreter* 10 (Autumn 1975): 133–40.

Hoshino, Akira. "The Future of Japanese Identity." Paper prepared for seminar, "The Challenge of Japan's Internationalization: Organization Culture," Kansei Gakuin University, June 30, 1981.

———. "An Elaboration of the 'Culture-Shock' Phenomenon: Adjustment Problems of Japanese Youth Returning from Overseas." In *Uprooting and Surviving*, ed. R. C. Nann. Dordrecht: D. Reidel, 1982.

Hyman, H. H. "Reflections on Reference Groups," *Public Opinion Quarterly* 24 (1960): 383–96.

Isajiw, Wsevolod W. "Definitions of Ethnicity." *Ethnicity* 1 (1974): 111–24.

Ishida, Eiichiro. "Japan Rediscovered." *Japan Quarterly* 11 (July–September 1964).

Jacobson, E. H. "Sojourn Research: A Definition of the Field." *Journal of Social Issues* 19 (1963): 123–29.

Jansen, Marius. "Modernization and Foreign Policy in Meiji Japan." In *Political Development in Modern Japan*, ed. R. Ward. Princeton, N.J.: Princeton University Press, 1968.

Karsh, Bernard, and Robert E. Cole. "Industrialization and the Convergence Hypothesis: Some Aspects of Contemporary Japan." *Journal of Social Issues* 4 (1968): 24.

Kato, Hidetoshi. "America as Seen by Japanese Travelers." In *Mutual Images*, ed. Akira Iriye. Cambridge, Mass.: Harvard University Press, 1975.

Kato, Katsuji. "Government Students from Japan." *Japanese Student* 5 (December 1916).

Kawai, Hayao. "Egalitarianism in Japanese Education." *Japan Echo* 2 (October 1975): 27–35.

Kiefer, Christie. "Personality and Social Change in a Japanese Danchi." Ph.D. diss., University of California at Berkeley, 1968.

———. "The Psychological Interdependence of Family, School and Bureaucracy in Japan." *American Anthropologist*, 72 (February 1970): 66–75.

Kikuiri, Ryusuke. "Shosha: Organizers of the World Economy." *Japan Interpreter* 8 (Autumn 1973): 353–73.

Kimoto, Wakako (Hironaka). "Adjustment of the Japanese Student to American Life." Master's thesis, Department of Sociology, Waltham, Mass.: Brandeis University, 1960.

Kitsuse, John I., Anne E. Murase, and Yoshoaki Yamamura. "Kikokushijo:

The Emergence and Institutionalization of an Educational Problem in Japan." In *Studies in the Sociology of Social Problems*, ed. Joseph W. Schneider and John I Kitsuse. New Jersey: Ablex Publishing Company, 1984, 162–79.

Klineberg, Otto. "A Science of National Character." *Journal of Social Psychology* 19 (1944): 147–62.

Kobayashi, Tetsuya. "Japan's Policy on Returning Students," *International Education and Cultural Exchange* 13 (Spring 1978).

———. "Adaptation of Overseas and Returning Children in Japan." Paper presented at Fourth World Congress of Comparative Education Society, Saitama, Japan, 1980.

———. "Educational Problems for Returning Children in Japan." In *Education and Social Concern: An Approach to Social Foundations*, ed. Robert F. Lawson, Val D. Rust, and Suzanne M. Shafer. Ann Arbor, Mich.: Prakken, 1987.

Kurihara, Akira. "The International Sense of the Japanese." *Japan Interpreter* (Summer–Autumn 1972).

La Brack, Bruce. "Internationalization: An Anti-Japanese Activity." *Japan Times* (August 7, 1983): 12.

Lambert, R. D., and Marvin Bressler. "The Sensitive-Area Complex: A Contribution to the Theory of Guided Culture Contact." *American Journal of Sociology* 60 (May 1955).

Lambert, R. D., and O. Klineberg. *Children's Views of Foreign Peoples*. New York: Appleton-Century-Crofts, 1967.

Lanham, Betty B. "Early Socialization: Stability and Change." *The Study of Japan in the Behavioral Sciences*, ed. E. Norbeck et al. *Rice University Studies* (Fall 1970): 322–33.

———. "The Mother-Child Relationship in Japan." *Monumenta Nipponica* 21 (1966).

Lee, Kiri. "Japan's 'Returning Children': Problems and Solutions." Master's thesis, Lesley College, Cambridge, Mass., 1982.

Le Vine, Robert A. "Socialization, Social Structure and Intersocietal Images." In *International Behavior: A Social-Psychological Analysis*, ed. H. Kelman. New York: Holt, Rinehart & Winston, 1965.

Lifton, Robert J. "Youth and History: Individual Change in Post-War Japan." *Daedalus* (Winter 1962) 172–97.

———. "Individual Patterns in Historical Change: Imagery of Japanese Youth." *Comparative Studies in Society and History* 6 (1964): 369–83.

———. "Protean Man." *Yale Alumni Review* (January 1969): 14–21.

Malkin, Martha, "Wholly-owned U.S. Subsidiaries in Japan and their Japanese Managers." A.B. diss., Harvard University, 1977.

Masui, Shigeo. "The Problem of the Comprehensive School in Japan." *International Review of Education* 17 (1971): 30–31.

Minami, Hiroshi. "The Introspection Boom." *Japan Interpreter* 8, (Spring 1973).

Ministry of Education. "Japan's Growth and Education: Educational Development in Relation to Socioeconomic Growth." In *Comparative Perspectives on Education*, ed. Robert J. Havighurst. Boston: Little, Brown, 1968.

Mishler, A. L. "Personal Contact in International Exchanges." In *Cross-National Encounters*, ed. Herbert C. Kelman and Raphael S. Ezekiel. San Francisco: Jossey-Bass, 1970.

Morris, H. C. "Ethnicity," *International Journal of the Social Sciences* 5 (1968).

Morris. R. "National Status and Attitudes of Foreign Students." *Journal of Social Issues* 12 (1956) 20–25.

Muro, Yoko. "How it Feels to be 'Not Quite' Japanese." *Japan Times* (March 27, 1983): 14.

Mushakoji, Kinhide. "The View from Japan." In *The United States and Japan*, ed. Herbert Passin. New York: Columbia University, 1966.

Muto, Toshiko. "Finding Identity: September Students at International Christian University." A.B. thesis, International Christian University, 1976.

Nagai, Michio. "Interview." *Look Japan* (April 1976).

———. "Are the Japanese 'International'?" *PHP* (July 1976): 53–65.

Nagai, Michio, and Takeo Nishijima. "Postwar Japanese Education and the United States." In *Mutual Images*, ed. Akira Iriye. Cambridge, Mass.: Harvard University Press, 1975.

Nagata, Judith A. "What is a Malay? Situational Selection of Ethnic Identity in a Plural Society." *American Ethnologist* 1 (May 1974).

Nambara, Shigeru. "The Ideals of Educational Reforms in Japan." *Educational Record* 31 (1950): 5–13.

Noel, Donald L. "A Theory of the Origin of Ethnic Stratification" *Social Problems* 16 (Fall 1968): 157–72.

Park, Robert E. "Behind Our Masks." *Survey* 56: 136.

———. "Human Migration and the Marginal Man." In *Race and Culture*, ed. Robert E. Park. Glencoe, Ill.: Free Press, 1950.

Parsons, Talcott. "Some Theoretical Aspects of the Problems of Ethnicity." (mimeo) Cambridge, Mass.

Passin, H., and J. W. Bennett. "The America-educated Japanese." *Annals of the American Academy of Political and Social Sciences* 295 (1954).

Perlmutter, Howard V. "Relations between the Self-Image, the Image of the Foreigner, and the Desire to Live Abroad." *Journal of Psychology* 38 (1954): 131–37.

Pool, Ithiel de Sola. "Effects of Cross-National Contact on National and International Images." In *Cross-National Encounters*, ed. Herbert C. Kelman. San Francisco: Jossey-Bass, 1970.

Ramsey, Charles E., and Robert J. Smith. "Japanese and American Perceptions of the Occupation." *American Journal of Sociology* 65 (1960): 475–82.

Riegel, Otto. "Residual Effects of Exchange of Persons." *Public Opinion Quarterly* 17 (1953): 319–27.

Riesman, David. "Japanese Intellectuals and Americans." *American Scholar* 1 (1964–5): 63.

Rohlen, Thomas P. "Is Japanese Education Becoming Less Egalitarian? Notes on High School Stratification and Reform." *Journal of Japanese Studies* (Winter 1976–77): 37–70.

————. "Permanent Employment Faces Recession, Slow Growth and an Aging Work Force." *Journal of Japanese Studies* 2 (Summer 1979): 235–72.

Schild, E. O. "The Foreign Student as Stranger, Learning the Norms of the Host-Culture." *Journal of Social Issues* 18 (1962): 41–54.

Shibutani, Tamotsu. "Reference Groups as Perspectives." *American Journal of Sociology* 60 (1955): 562–70.

Shils, E. "Primordial, Personal, Sacred and Civil Ties." *British Journal of Sociology* 8 (June 1957): 130–45.

Shimizu, Yoshihiro. "Entrance Examinations: A Challenge to Equal Opportunity in Education." *Journal of Social and Political Ideas in Japan* 1 (December 1963): 88–93.

Siegel, Bernard J. "Social Structure, Social Change and Education in Rural Japan: A Case Study." In *Education and Culture-Anthropological Approaches*, ed. George Spindler. New York: Holt, Rinehart & Winston, 1963.

Sikkema, Mildred. "Observations of Japanese Early Child Training." In *Personal Character and Cultural Milieu*, ed. D. Haring. Syracuse N.Y.: Syracuse University Press, 1948.

Simmel, Georg. "The Sociological Significance of the Stranger." In *Introduction to the Science of Sociology*, R. E. Park, ed. Chicago: University of Chicago Press, 1921.

Singleton, John. "Urban-Rural Comparisons in Japanese Education." *International Review of Education* 13 (1967): 470–82.

Smith, Howard P. "Do Intercultural Experiences Affect Attitudes?" *Journal of Abnormal Social Psychology* 51 (1955): 469–77.

Smith, Robert J. "The Japanese Rural Community: Norms, Sanctions and Ostracism." *American Anthropologist* (1961): 522–33.

Spicer, E. "Persistent Cultural Systems." *Science* 174, (November 19, 1971): 795–800.

Swartz, M. J. "Negative Ethnocentrism." *Journal of Conflict Resolution* 5 (1961): 75–81.

Takane, Masaaki. "Readjusting to a Uniformed Society." *Japan Interpreter* 10 (Autumn 1975): 208–210.

Tsurumi, Yoshi. Oil Crisis: The Japanese Context. *Daedalus* (Fall 1975): 113–27.

————. "Multiculturalism and Management: Incorporating Employees' Interest in Corporate Objectives." Paper presented at the annual meeting of the Canadian Association of Administrative Sciences, Toronto, (June 2–4, 1979).

Tsuruta, Chieko. "Effects of Cross-National Contact: A Case Study of Returnee Children Who Have Lived in the United States." A.B. thesis, Sophia University, Tokyo, 1976.

Umesao, Tadao. "Escape from Cultural Isolation." *Japan Interpreter* (September 1974): 133–48.

Utsurikawa, Nenozo. "The Status of Japanese Students in America Past and Present." *Education* 33 (November 1912): 144–49.

Vogel, Ezra F. "The Social Base of Japan's Post-War Economic Growth." In U.S. *International Economic Policy in an Interdependent World*. Washington, D.C.: Government Printing Office, 1971.

Vogel, Suzanne. "The Professional Housewife." *Japan Interpreter* 12 (Autumn 1978): 16–43.

Vogel, Suzanne. "Toward Understanding the Adjustment Problems of Foreign Families in the College Community," Harvard University Health Services, 1985.

Watanabe, Osamu. "On Returning from Southeast Asia." *Japan Quarterly* 22:1 (January–March 1975).

Weiner, Myron. "Political Integration and Political Development." *Annals of the American Academy of Political Science* 358 (March 1965): 52–64.

White, Merry I. "Entrance Examinations." *Encyclopedia of Japan* (1981).

Wirth, Louis. "Types of Nationalism." *American Journal of Sociology* 41 (1936): 723–37.

Yamakawa, Sutematsu. "First Impressions of Japan After Eleven Years' Absence in America." *Independent* 5 (March 8, 1833): 290–91.

Yang, C. K. "Chinese Bureaucratic Behavior." In *Confucianism in Action,* eds. David S. Nivison and Arthur F. Wright, Palo Alto: Stanford University Press, 1959.

Yoshiko, Sato. "Facing Silent Society: The Maladjustment of Japanese Returning Children." Paper prepared for Harvard Graduate School of Education, 1982.

Yoshino, M. Y. "Emerging Japanese Multinational Enterprises." In *Modern Japanese Organizations and Decision-Making,* ed. Ezra F. Vogel. Berkeley: University of California Press, 1975.

―――. "Showa-Packard Ltd." Case Study. Cambridge: Harvard Business School, 1973.

Zimmerman, Mark. *How to Do Business with the Japanese.* New York: Random House, 1985.

Japanese Language Sources

Aida Yuji. "Kosei aru kuni" (A unique country) *PHP* (Fall 1969) 5–22.

Aizawa Toni. "Gaikokujin to hanashio shitai kedo . . . " (I want to talk with foreigners, but . . .). *PHP* (Winter 1976).

Gakugei Daigaku Fuzoku Oizumi Chugakko. *Kikoku Shijo Kyoiku . . .* (The education of returnee children). Tokyo, 1975.

Gengo Seikatsu. Special issue. *Gaikokujin no tame no Nihongo Kyoiku 279* (Japanese language education for foreigners), 1974.

Ishida Eiichiro. "Nipponjin no ijin ishiki" (Japanese attitudes toward foreigners). *USHIO* (August 1967): 78–86.

Ministry of Education. *Kaigai Shijo Kyoiku no suido ni kansuru konponteki shisaku ni tsuite* (Concerning basic thoughts on educating children overseas). Tokyo, 1976.

Japan Air Lines Family Service. *Akarui Kaigai Seikatsu no tame ni* (For a bright life overseas). Tokyo: JAL Publications, 1974.

―――. *Okosama o kaigai de sodateru tame ni* (How to raise children overseas). Tokyo: JAL Publications, annual.

―――. *Amerika kara kikoku kazoku no hoo e* (For the families returning from America). Tokyo: JAL Publications, monthly magazine, 1975–78.

―――. *Kaigai no seikatsu no shiori* (A guide to life overseas). Tokyo: JAL Publications, 1975.

―――. *Kikoku o mimae ni hikaete* (Looking toward the return home). Tokyo: JAL Publications, monthly magazine, 1975–80.

Kaigai Shijo Kyoiku Shinko Zaidan. *Kaigai Shijo Kyoiku* (The Education of Children Overseas). Tokyo, monthly periodical 1975–80.

Kanayama Norio. *Kokusai Tekiogaku Nyūmon* (Introduction to the science of international adaptology). Tokyo: Simul Press, 1971.

Kato Kyoko. Amerika e itta Ryoko (Ryoko who went to America). Tokyo: Asahi Shimbunsha, 1975.

Kato Shuichi. *Nihon no uchi to soto* (The concepts of "inside" and "outside" in Japan). Tokyo: Bungei Shunjusha, 1968.

Keimei Gakuen. *Kaigai Zaikin no kata no Shijo no kyoiku ni tsuite* (Concerning the education of the children overseas). Tokyo, 1975.

Kikoku Shijo Kyoiku (The Education of Returning Children). *New York OCS News*. November 15, 1975.

Kimata Shinichi and Kimata Mitsu. *Tsumetai shakai, Atatakai Shakai* (Cold society, warm society). Tokyo: Simul Press, 1973.

Kitadai Junji. "Haikei, Nagai Monbudaijin domo" (Dear Education Minister Nagai . . .). *Bungei Shunju* (May 1975): 164–78.

Koike Ijuo. "Kaigai ni okeru Nihonjin chūzaiin no dōtai to eigo shokku." (Statistics on Japanese in residence abroad and their "English shock"). *ELEC Bulletin* (Spring–Summer 1976).

Nagai Michio. "Eigo wa Nihon de Manaberu" (Can One Learn English in Japan?) *The English Journal* 3 (March 1973).

Nihon Kokusai Koryu Center. *Kokusai Kyoiku* (International Education). Tokyo, monthly magazine, 1975–82.

Ogiyama S. *Umi o wataru Kodomotachi* (Children who cross the seas). Tokyo: Kaigai Shijo Kyoiku Shinko Zaidan, 1976.

Shiroyama Saburō. *Mainichi ga Nichiyobi*. [Everyday is Sunday] Tokyo: Shincho Press, 1976.

Sono Kazuhiko. *Kaigai de Kodomo o sodateru oya no yomuhon*. (A Primer for Parents Raising Children Overseas). Tokyo, 1975.

Sugiyama Junko et al. *Kodomo no kokoro to karada o dō sodateru ka?* (How should we care for our children's minds and bodies?). Tokyo: JAL World, 1975.

Takane Masaaki. "Kogakureki jidai no kyoso genri." (Principles of competition in an age requiring high academic backgrounds). *Chuo Koron* (July 1975): 58–72.

Tanu Koichi and Tanu Nobuko. *Kizudarake no kodomotachi* (The wounded children). Tokyo: Mainichi, 1976.

Index